ONE
PLUS
ONE
EQUALS
ONE

THE WORLD'S
GREATEST LOVE
RELATIONSHIP
EQUATION

TONY & SHIRLEY SCOTT

One + One = One
© 2021 by Tony and Shirley Scott

Published by Insight International, Inc.
contact@freshword.com
www.freshword.com
918-493-1718

Unless otherwise noted all Scripture quotations are taken from the Amplified® Bible. Copyright © 2015 by The Lockman Foundation, La Habra, CA 90631. Used by permission. www.Lockman.org.

Scripture quotations marked (TPT) are from The Passion Translation®. Copyright © 2017, 2018, 2020 by Passion & Fire Ministries, Inc. Used by permission. All rights reserved. ThePassionTranslation.com.

Scripture quotations marked (NIV) are from THE HOLY BIBLE, NEW INTERNATIONAL VERSION®, NIV®. Copyright © 1973, 1978, 1984, 2011 by Biblica, Inc.® Used by permission. All rights reserved worldwide.

Scripture quotations marked (NKJV) are from the New King James Version®. Copyright © 1982 by Thomas Nelson. Used by permission. All rights reserved.

Scripture quotations marked (MSG) are from *THE MESSAGE*. Copyright © 1993, 2002, 2018 by Eugene H. Peterson. Used by permission of NavPress. All rights reserved. Represented by Tyndale House Publishers, Inc.

Scripture quotation marked (KJV) is taken from the King James Version of the Bible.

Scripture quotation marked (NLT) is taken from the *Holy Bible,* New Living Translation. Copyright © 1996, 2004, 2015 by Tyndale House Foundation. Used by permission of Tyndale House Publishers, Inc., Carol Stream, Illinois 60188. All rights reserved.

Scripture quotations marked (AMPC) are from the Amplified® Bible (AMPC). Copyright © 1954, 1958, 1962, 1964, 1965, 1987 by The Lockman Foundation. Used by permission. www.Lockman.org.

Paperback ISBN: 978-1-943361-84-7
Hardback ISBN: 978-1-943361-85-4
E-Book ISBN: 978-1-943361-86-1

Library of Congress Control Number: 2021907472

Printed in the United States of America.

"For this reason a man shall leave his father and his mother and shall be joined [and be faithfully devoted] to his wife, and the two shall become one flesh" (Ephesians 5:31).

Endorsements

There is no doubt that marriages are under attack, especially in the church, and ***One + One = One*** by Tony and Shirley Scott will impart truths only found in 55 years of marriage.

JENTEZEN FRANKLIN
Senior Pastor, Free Chapel
New York Times Best-Selling Author

In this book ***One + One = One,*** Pastor Tony Scott and his wife ShirleyAnn undeniably bring across a deep and life-changing understanding of the foundational truth God has given His children to live by—one flesh. We can think of no greater message for husbands and wives everywhere at this junction in humanity's history.

MARCUS and JONI LAMB
President and Founders, Daystar Television Network

One of the most fiercely debated, contentious, and often scorned institutions in America today is marriage. Marriage is the hot-button issue of our time, which is why Tony and Shirley Scott's new book, ***One + One = One***: *The World's Greatest Love Relationship Equation* is so important. First—it's a powerful and touching tribute to an amazing marriage; but just as vital, it's the perspective we need at this cultural moment. I had the opportunity to work with Tony and Shirley and saw their remarkable relationship in action. Their lives had far more impact when they stood side by side, and every day they showed us what a great marriage could be. Get this book. It's the kind of story we don't hear about in today's polarized media, but it's a book that will leave a lasting legacy.

PHIL COOKE, Ph.D.
Author, Media Producer, and Founder of
Cooke Media Group

One + One = One is an epic manuscript of the beautiful six-decade love story of Pastor Tony and Shirley Scott, but it is much more than just a story. It is a true gift and a tool that has been given to the Kingdom at such a critical time in our culture and society. It will not just speak to the individual or couple about living a blessed and prosperous life, but it will be a compass and a road map to help you navigate through difficult seasons. The Scotts have truly loved, lived, and embodied these Kingdom principles and found the secret to becoming *"one."* This book will bless and speak life to anyone who reads it.

TONY and KACI STEWART
Lead Pastors, Citylife Church, Tampa, Florida

One + One = One is the incredible story of Tony and Shirley Scott's 55-year marriage that found its strength in Jesus Christ and in their selfless commitment to each other. Get ready for an emotional journey. Tony and Shirley's lives and love teach us what "for better, for worse, for richer, for poorer, in sickness and in health, to love and to cherish, until death do us part" really means. Whether you're single, engaged, married, or widowed, we all have important lessons to learn from this book.

SAMMY RODRIGUEZ
President, National Hispanic Christian Leadership
Conference (NHCLC)

Every believer and certainly every married couple need to read, experience, and live *One + One = One*. I could hardly stop reading this deep and sometimes raw story of Pastor Tony and Shirley's 58-year life journey, where God let them experience life and challenge to the fullest, and how He showed them the way to overcome was together. Chapter after chapter of Pastor Tony and Shirley's words of intentional love and commitment give us lessons to live by on our own journeys and an example to follow and duplicate.

CHAD CONNELLY
President, Faith Wins

Reading the love story of Tony and Shirley was captivating. Truth be told, almost everyone who reads this book has suffered great loss, losses from which we never fully recover. It is this point that causes me to encourage everyone to read this book. Tony and Shirley's love was exceptional. What will this book do for you? Firstly, it is the model that high school and college students need to read to understand the joy of pure, Christ-honoring courtship. Secondly, it can become a model for countless married couples who could learn so much from the pristine love of Tony and Shirley.

Dr. JIM GARLOW
CEO, Well Versed

One + One = One is one of the best books about marital relationships that you will ever read! It is an autobiography of an amazing journey of love that is tested through hardship and trials, including the endurance and faith needed when physical suffering hits your one true love. Each chapter reveals powerful truths that will inspire your mind and spirit. Tony and Shirley were inseparable, only by death. There are times in life you will experience things that just don't add up. Yet, it is all a part of the life process. Those experiences that make us who we are. You will learn from this book why One + One really does just equal One!

PERRY STONE
Founder, Voice of Evangelism Ministries

The Scriptures reveal a principle for the marriage relationship. Tony Scott and ShirleyAnn effectively reveal that principle in this book *One + One = One*. I've had the unique privilege of watching their marriage and ministry lived out according to that principle. My own wife, Kelly, grew up under their teaching and leadership. Our lives and marriage have been enriched and strengthened because of God's Truth, and because of the living letters we've both witnessed in their marriage. *One + One = One* is a must-read for every couple who wants to live under a pronounced blessing of unity in God's design for the marriage relationship.

TRAVIS JOHNSON
Pastor, Pathway Church

Dedication

"BEAUTY is in the eye of the beholder."

To behold ShirleyAnn Scott was to love her. With a radiant smile that would light up any room and a personality manifesting warm southern charm, people from all walks of life were drawn to her. Words of acceptance, affirmation, and approval flowed from her heart, adding value to the listener. ShirleyAnn was first and foremost a lover of God and of others, and she delighted in showering encouragement on those wounded by life's challenges.

As a woman, she led from a position of strength—always confident in her own skin, knowing her true identity. Intelligence, street smarts, wisdom, and simple common sense caused confidence to emanate from within.

As a wife, she excelled in loving me, inspiring me, coaching me, and serving as my filter and anchor. She knew how I wanted to be loved and needed to be affirmed. I needed her because I loved her.

As a mother and grandmother, she was loving yet strong. Darin and Melony experienced generous affirmations as well as strong corrections. Olivia, Bella, Mackenzie, and Abbie felt her passion for God and desire for them to serve Him as she did.

As a pastor's wife, she weathered the storms with worship and devotion. Her love for Jesus was passionate as she walked in covenant with Him. She could say with Paul, "For me to live is Christ and to die is gain." And she did both.

ShirleyAnn was my life—the love of my life and the life of my love.

Proverbs 31:28-31 (TPT)

Her sons and daughters arise in one accord to extol her virtues,
  and her husband arises to speak of her in glowing terms.
There are many valiant and noble ones,
  but you have ascended above them all!
 ...this virtuous woman lives in the wonder, awe,
  and fear of the Lord.
She will be praised *throughout eternity.*
So go ahead and give her the credit that is due,
  for she has become a radiant woman,
  and all her loving works of righteousness deserve
  to be admired
  at the gateways of every city!

This book was in her heart for many years. It is her living legacy to marriages everywhere. We are **One** + **One** = **One** forever.

To you, my beautiful, faithful, loving God-sent wife, I dedicate ***One + One = One.***

Contents

Foreword

AND the two shall become one.

These six powerful Words from Mark 10 are ingrained in the believer as the quintessential plan for a husband and wife. It is the epitome of a Christ-centered marriage, where two people come together and are "one flesh," and is perhaps the most powerful description of life-long commitment between a man and a woman. When I was asked to pen this foreword it came without hesitation as I can think of no other couple that best demonstrates this biblical principle than Tony and Shirley Scott. I knew from observing the Scotts for decades that their model of Christian servanthood, partnership in ministry, commitment to one another, and unparalleled love was an example of which every couple should endeavor to emulate.

Tony and Shirley Scott's **One + One** relationship reminds me of Psalm 133, "Behold, how good and how pleasant it is for brothers to dwell together in unity! It is like the precious oil upon the head...." Their unity as a couple was like precious oil, as it was poured out upon those around them when they ministered together for decades in Toledo. I recall when they took the church as a young couple, basically relaunching a struggling congregation to turn it into an influence for Christ, not just in Toledo, but around the globe. As fellow pastors, who have also endured challenges and triumphs, our friendship with Tony and Shirley remained priceless. Leading with Tony as members of the International Executive Council for a major Pentecostal denomination was a privilege.

Shirley Scott was purely Pentecostal, the daughter of a minister, and a pastor's wife. She was the Proverbs 31 woman, serving at home and giving life-long care and influence to their children, Darin and Melony. Shirley's children rise up to call her blessed. Her character was loving and effervescent, never meeting a stranger, and always finding ways to promote her husband in ministry. At the same time, she was a minister in her own right, working as an integral part of the leadership and operations of the church. I was honored to witness her becoming credentialed as an ordained minister in the denomination in which Tony and I serve. She took that title seriously as a tool to lead even more effectively.

Every couple—particularly those in ministry—needs to read *One + One = One*. It's the whole package, starting with the first day they met. After that, you didn't see one without knowing the other was nearby. She was never behind him, but beside him. It includes happy times, challenges, tragedies, and victories. The phrase **One + One = One** is woven throughout its twelve chapters, each of which concludes with an examination of the "oneisms." It features word-for-word entries from their personal journals. While its publication came after Shirley's untimely passing, she is truly the co-author. Tony's intensely candid thoughts shared in the final chapters about losing his soulmate serve as a spiritual and emotional road map for recovery.

Quoting Tony's own words, he sums it up: "Because of the principle of oneness we learned and lived, my life is still benefiting since she is so totally ingrained in my DNA. Forever, it will be **One + One = One**."

Dr. TIM HILL
General Overseer of the Church of God

Why This Book?

A relational equation that can transform your life

SOWN into the Universe is a profound principle that affects every person. Whenever commerce, sports, corporations, marriages, or families activate this law it brings greater focus, unity, togetherness, and production than could otherwise be achieved. It is an eternal law and powerfully effective in all human relationships. It very well could be the most overlooked principle in creation. God combined it with the permanence of covenant in the very first marriage. Simply put, it is called the Law of Oneness. Brought into any relationship the impact is profound and exponential.

From the day Shirley and I met until her last day on this Earth, we were blessed to truly be one. We desire that all who read this book experience the **treasure of true love, the mystery of oneness,** and the **secret of a covenant life** while understanding that sometimes the **answers don't come.** Be prepared to confront, with true ancient wisdom, some of the shallow and accepted norms of creating great relationships. These truths transformed our married life from ordinary to extraordinary, from just "being married" to a covenant marriage. Our love never stopped growing and the passion to be part of each other's life was ever-increasing. We were best friends until the end. The principles we discovered in our 55-year marriage can revolutionize your relationships as well. Are you ready to take your relationship to the next level?

With us, life became **One + One = One**. Being together 24/7, year after year, was one of the greatest blessings we experienced. However, on August 18th, 2020 at 4:05 a.m., ShirleyAnn Lesley Scott slipped the bonds of human flesh to awaken in the Presence of Jesus Christ. It was her heart's desire for us to write a book together which would help struggling couples such as ourselves on this journey of faith. The shock of her leaving turned my world upside down. But because of the principle of oneness we learned and lived, my life is still benefiting since she is so totally ingrained in my DNA. Forever, it will be **One + One = One**.

Introduction

Oneness . . . something you must experience

LIFE is filled with secrets and mysteries that are discovered on our earthly journey. Shirley felt strongly about sharing our true love story to let people see the triumphs, the struggles, the victories, the conflicts, the ups and downs, and the beauty of a growing, maturing relationship.

Repeatedly, in the course of our lives, there are things we wish we had known. Shirley and I often thought of writing a book, sharing our hearts, and letting people see the good, the challenging, the whatever side of life. For more than 50 years, God has permitted us to serve His Kingdom. During that time, we were blessed beyond words by loving, generous, God-fearing, Kingdom-minded relationships. If only someone could have written a book like this many years ago, perhaps we would have gained much-needed wisdom that we often lacked. However, we learned that the weapons of our warfare were uniquely revealed to us by God in times of need. Scripture vividly portrays our lives as being individually important to God, and thus no two people fight the good fight of faith exactly alike. While books can help teach us ways of perfecting our lives with certain biblical principles, for us, experience was a great teacher. It enlarged our faith and made us totally dependent on His grace. Get ready for an amazing journey as together we walk you through half a century of watching God show up when others did not, of watching Him provide grace, of watching Him come through. Amazing grace is an appropriate title, not just of a song, but for how grace works in relationships. It only shows up at the point of need. We learned that there is never pre-grace. Her prayer, as well as mine, is that your life will be profoundly impacted by the uniqueness of our journey. Shirley was a multi-gifted and very special servant of God. Totally unselfish in the way she lived, she always believed the best in everyone. Her servant heart came shining through every time she met someone who was hurting or in need. It was always our prayer that our unique journey and passionate marriage relationship could make yours more meaningful and fulfilling. The principle of **One** + **One** = **One** is the world's greatest relational truth. Just like a math equation, wherever you find people in a relationship, this Law of Oneness can be utilized to exponentially increase the effectiveness of the relationship.

> The principle of *One + One = One* is the world's greatest relationship truth.

One Life Is Not Enough to Live With You

July 9, 2015

You were, are, and always will be an amazing woman. Together we have traversed this ministry-calling highway no matter where it led us. Always you have given it your all. Most people only see the "glory" of ministry—you and I know the pain and disappointment that often goes with it. You, more than I, have suffered greatly these last few years. With every step, your life revealed the depth of your covenant love for Jesus. How I wish it would have been me! You have never lost that intoxicating smile, that never-give-up attitude, and that dogged determination to outlast the attack. We have purposely tried to live our lives without regrets. When this journey ends, I will have one regret—that I did not have more than one life to live with you! You are the love of my life and the life of my love! Happy 50th Anniversary, Shirley!

Part 1:

Treasure of True Love

Chapter 1

The Beginning of Us

"YOU want to drive over to Greenville with me and check out the girls at youth camp?" my friend David asked.

"Sure, why not?" I replied.

It was June 1962. As we pulled into the parking lot and drove by the concession stands, I saw two people standing out front.

I asked David, "Who is the brown-haired girl?"

He replied, "It's Shirley Lesley, and you don't have a chance."

That's like saying "sic 'em to a pit bull!"

As we approached the two of them, she introduced herself: "I'm Shirley."

"I'm Tony," I replied.

Little did I realize at that moment, this day would change my life forever.

I was fifteen years old when I met Tony at a summer church camp. My girlfriend and I were standing near the refreshment stand as two young men came walking toward us across the parking lot.

I remember saying, "Wow! Who is that guy?"

They came closer and Tony and I began to talk, all the while not knowing our destiny was just beginning. When I asked Tony his future plans, he commented, "I want to be a businessman and own my own business." I said, "Good, you are just the guy I've been looking for."

Without knowing it, we were on the same spiritual path.

That was the beginning of us—a 58-year journey which became a love story for the ages. I continued to go back that week just to see her. In just four weeks, the annual Church of God camp meeting would convene on the same grounds. Since her dad was a pastor, I knew they would be there. When youth camp was over that week, she asked when we could see one another again. We were determined to meet the week of camp meeting. I drove over every night, and we attended the services. Our first official date was on Sunday, July 2. She insisted I dress up in a suit and tie. She had on a yellow dress and hat. Undoubtedly, she was the most beautiful girl I had ever seen. Neither of us wanted that night to end since she was such a long distance away—all of 50 miles. Several weeks passed and the Church of God General Assembly was convened in Texas. Her dad was appointed to a church in Iva, South Carolina—only 15 miles from my house in Anderson. We had talked a few times on the phone, and the first day they arrived in Iva, she called to ask if I could come and see her. At the time, I didn't possess a vehicle, so I had to borrow one from my brother or sister. Upon arriving at her home in Iva, I rang the doorbell, and she opened the door. My hair was rather long, but I had since gotten a crew cut.

First words out of her mouth: "What happened to your hair?"

To which I replied, "I got a crew cut."

She laughed and started to close the door. "Come back when it starts to grow out."

That was Shirley. Amazing wit and humor. She reopened the door and welcomed me in.

From the very start of our true love story, it was obvious God had brought us together. With no car of my own, I was constantly borrowing one.

Owning my own vehicle hit a snag when I was involved in an accident.

Just two years earlier, on a Wednesday night, I was driving to the McDuffie Street Church for service along with my mom and sister. As we drove up Murray Ave, a man came walking across the median and into the path of my car. He went flying through the air and landed face down on the pavement. All of us got out of the car and were shocked at what had happened. As he lay on the road in a pool of blood, I knew it was serious. After the ambulance drove away with him, we proceeded to the church. Mom had the pastor talk and pray with me. For three days, the man lingered between life and death. On that Sunday morning after service, I walked out of church and started down the long steps to see my sister just getting out of her car. I could tell she was crying.

I asked, "Did he die?"

She nodded her head.

Crumbling to my knees on those concrete steps, I began to sob. I was guilty of hitting a man with my vehicle who later died. My sister went in and got the pastor who brought me to the front seat to pray with me. There was a coroner's inquest, and the ruling was "accident." We later learned this man was blind on the right side. When he was walking across the street, he never saw me. Nonetheless, I would have nightmares concerning what happened. In addition, the lack of insurance on the vehicle resulted in my license being suspended for six months. The insurance was now sky high, and I certainly couldn't afford to purchase a vehicle.

I learned a very valuable lesson—it's not what happens to you that determines the course of your way, but what happens within you. This tragedy caused me to rededicate my life to Christ, instead of being a nominal Christian. Challenges in life are permitted by God to stretch us and reveal to us the God potential that is within. God uses whatever happens to us—whether good, bad, ugly, or beautiful—to bring out the God-given purpose within us.

Then a break came, and I secured a job working third shift at Singer Corporation. It was a production job, and I began to earn quite a bit of money because I worked fast. Soon, I bought a 1964 VW Beetle. It was brand new and very good on gas. From that moment on, I was back and forth to see her four to five times a week. Even then, it was like we were together all the time, but still not together enough. She was entering the tenth grade; I was at Anderson University, and her parents insisted she graduate before she could marry.

From our beginning as a couple, we determined our relationship would be God-honoring, and we would keep it pure. Never did we regret that decision. Working third shift, I would often leave Iva and go straight to work at 11 p.m. This went on for three years. During those years, it was Tony and Shirley. We were an item—almost always together, and everyone knew we were getting married as soon as she graduated from high school.

Shirley was very popular in high school, and she was chosen as the *Future Farmers of America Sweetheart.* An argument arose between us because I didn't like her being photographed with one of the guys in the group, but our arguments never lasted. I was proud of her knowing she was first of all *my* sweetheart. Even then, there was a spirit of oneness about our relationship which we most likely didn't fully grasp at that time. Remaining angry was not something either of us could do.

There would be other challenges to our relationship. However, she and I were developing an intentional true love affair—I intended to love her regardless, she intended to love me regardless. Intentional love is not just a matter of the heart, it is also a matter of will. Being "in love" is not enough to build a relationship on, let alone a marriage. In this early stage of our true love romance, even without our knowledge, we were beginning to understand what **One + One = One** really meant. In later years, that principle would propel us into His Kingdom work. Looking back over our lives after Shirley passed into the arms of Jesus, I began to understand a great truth—**Life is lived looking forward but understood as you look back.**

Intentional love is only accomplished at the core of your being— not on the surface. It requires focus, commitment, and resolve that the relationship will never end.

While we were dating, quite often we sat on the living room couch while her parents were in the den. Shortly before 11 p.m., her dad would bang on the wall, and I knew it was time for me to leave. Their house in Iva faced the road and had a picture window with drapes always pulled open. When I got ready to go home, I would pull the drapes closed so I could kiss her goodnight. Then she would open the drapes back up, so her parents wouldn't know what happened. One neighbor noticed the drapes were closed and asked her parents about it.

Shirley simply told them, "You don't want everyone seeing us kiss, do you?"

Iva was a very small town with little to do, so we often drove back to Anderson for dates—15 miles there, 15 miles back. We put a lot of miles on the VW. Neither of us can really remember discussing getting married; we just knew we were meant for each other. I did ask her dad if I could marry his daughter one day, and he agreed.

After two years of dating, we actually broke up because I didn't think her dad liked me. Of course, there were a few other things.... One Wednesday night, a buddy of mine, Tommy, asked me to get something to eat at McDonald's. His girlfriend was in the front, so I sat in the back. One of her friends came up to the car as we sat at McDonald's. She was having issues with her boyfriend and needed some counseling. She got into the backseat where I was. At the same time, a group of kids from Iva came to that McDonald's, and Shirley was with them. While I was talking with this young lady, Tommy went to get our food.

Shirley met him and asked, "Is that Tony in your backseat?"

When he came back to the car and handed me my food, he said, "I think your career in Iva just got shot all to _ _ _ _."

One thing should be made clear—this girl was not my date. She got into the car where I was. Even then, the pastoral gift was present, and I was ministering to her. You can't fault me for that. (Seriously!) Later, I called Shirley and her mother answered. She told me that Shirley didn't want to speak to me. I begged; Shirley refused, so I got my mother out of bed to talk to her mom. My mom asked to speak to Shirley (she always loved my mom), and she came to the phone. Mom explained this girl was one of Tommy's friends, and I was not dating her. My mom made it clear I was very upset and desperately needed her to talk to me. Our breakup was short-lived, and we were back on track in no time. We knew these small conflicts wouldn't stand in our way for what was inevitable.

There wasn't money for a big wedding, so my mom and I went to work in a sewing factory to earn enough to buy material for my dress, flowers, and food for the wedding. Tony was always the resourceful one. Since he was a newspaper carrier for many years, he remembered *The Anderson Independent* had a "Bride of the Month," which included a free honeymoon to Jacksonville, Florida.

8

He knew the people inside and convinced them it would be great if one of their paper carriers was given that "Bride of the Month" recognition. They agreed and took several pictures of me for the newspaper. And there I was all dressed up in my beautiful dress for the 9th of July 1965.

A prominent German scholar once said concerning
marriage, "Here is to matrimony—the high sea adventure
for which no compass has yet been invented."

Here we are...two very young people about to become one in a marriage covenant we probably do not understand. After all, we had been single our entire lives. However, we entered this marriage relationship determined to have the best marriage possible. Being familiar with the story of Adam and Eve and the first wedding in the

Garden, it seems that we were bright-eyed about the beauty, power, and blessing of the two of us becoming one. Having saved ourselves for each other, we came into the marriage relationship with great expectations of what it would offer us. In Genesis, God formed the man from the dust of the ground, and He made the woman from a rib in Adam's side. "Formed" means to fashion as a potter would a vessel. Perhaps God was saying something about a man pursuing his purpose and being consumed with it since a pot usually is filled with one thing at a time. On the other hand, He made the woman, which refers to the building of a palace, a temple, or forms of art. Joining the man to the woman in a covenant of God under His grand purpose, a whole new world is revealed to them.

When you see a pair of scissors, there are two blades, two components that are joined and never to be separated. The blades frequently go in different directions, but they are most powerful and most productive when they come together. It is then that the scissors fulfill their purpose. The same goes with oneness in marriage.

Discovering who you really are is one of life's most empowering experiences. The way two people come together in a marriage relationship is often hindered for lack of understanding who they are. Knowing "who" you are is very important, especially before choosing a mate. He devised, formed our destiny, our intended purpose, our true identity. Don't ask yourself what the world needs. Ask yourself what makes you come alive and go do that because what the world needs is people who are fully alive and truly know "who" they are.

Individually, we desire someone to know us thoroughly and accept us unconditionally. Getting to know your spouse is a long and wonderful process, or not. The best thing is to learn from each other and to celebrate your differences. No two people are ever going to come to the place in a marriage where they are exactly alike in the way they think, act, and speak. The main difference between men and women is that they think differently. Every couple needs to learn how to appreciate their differences. From the very beginning, Shirley and I learned to communicate with each other and found out communication breeds intimacy.

When we came home at night from working during the day, we talked about what went on. I knew about the people at the bank (even then, Shirley was trying to help a woman with her marriage), and she knew about my classes at Anderson College, as well as my job as a retail sales rep. Shirley always wanted to know every detail, every day of my life, and I tried to be interested in the details of hers. In those early days, we had some challenges with our strong personalities but seemed to always find a way to talk through them. Without realizing what we were doing, we actually learned how to have a fight, a disagreement. Our most important discovery? Issues and persons are two different things. So, we didn't make it personal. She didn't attack me, and I didn't attack her. We focused on the issue—something we had to learn and practice.

Always remember: once you speak a word you have given it life, and you can never kill it. You may say, "I'm sorry, I didn't mean that. I wish I had not said that," (and you will wish you hadn't said it) but a spoken word is given life and nothing can cause its death. We learned that words can affirm, add value, and build up, or they can injure, tear down, and decrease someone. When you intentionally love someone, you want to be forever adding value to their lives. Our life was pure, passionate, and growing. Something very magnetic was drawing us closer to each other. Continuously, we were becoming one and loving every minute of it. Of course, that required some adjustments, as we were two very strong personalities. However, we always enjoyed making up. We were **One + One = Becoming One**.

And this was the beginning of us....

Oneisms from Chapter 1

- ♥ It's not what happens to you that determines the course of your way, but what happens within you.

- ♥ Intentional love is not just a matter of the heart, it is also a matter of will.

- ♥ Life is lived looking forward but understood as you look back.

- ♥ Be intentional in your marriage relationship and be determined it will be the best it can be.

- ♥ Discovering who you really are is one of life's most empowering experiences.

- ♥ We desire someone to know us thoroughly and accept us unconditionally.

- ♥ The best thing is to learn from each other and celebrate your differences.

- ♥ Always remember: once you speak a word you have given it life, and you can never kill it.

Chapter 2

Discovering Married Love

IN life, you must discover who you really are; never permit someone else or something else to determine that for you. When God brought Shirley and me together, He knew who we were, even if we did not. It was my goal to do something in business, perhaps own a business, make a good amount of money, and have a good life. Shirley's goal was not to marry a minister because she didn't like moving around from church to church as her parents had done all those years. Over the next few years, we settled into our new home, 205 Sandlewood Drive in Anderson, South Carolina. A friend of mine who was a contractor had built it for himself and his wife. Although I didn't have a full-time job, he helped me get a loan at the bank, so I could purchase the house that was only six months old. I had saved up $1,000 as a down payment, and her mom and dad were pretty impressed.

Not long after we were married, I was headed home at six in the morning after delivering papers for the local newspaper. Driving home, in front of Anderson University, a patrolman came out of nowhere, lights flashing, and pulled me over. Walking up to my car, shining the flashlight in my face, he asked for my license. It should be noted I was not speeding this time!

He said, "I'm sure you are wondering why I pulled you over," to which I replied, "Yes, I am."

"The Holiday Inn on Main Street was robbed a short time ago and over the scanner, it was reported to be a blue vehicle and a guy in a gray coat."

I was driving a blue vehicle and I was wearing a gray coat, but I can assure you I did not rob the Holiday Inn. (Now a bank? Maybe. The extra cash would have been nice!) He followed me back to the Holiday Inn, took me inside, and asked the desk clerk if I matched the description of the person who robbed him.

Obviously, the clerk said "No," and I was free to go.

On my way home that morning and for many years to come, three questions would linger in my mind: Who am I? What am I? and Why am I? Being in college at the time, as well as working a job, there never seemed to be a time for that discussion. Shirley and I were in love, and we only needed each other. She was my world, and I was her world. We truly had no clue as to where we were headed. Actually, we were very "surface people"— not realizing the treasure God had buried inside of us. Not only was the patrolman guilty of mistaken identity, but I also felt at times the same was true for me. At this time, my marriage caused me to put everything else on the back burner. There was no time to dig deeper. However, soon we would learn the hidden treasure of our true love had not been discovered.

Shirley made our new house a dream home. Little by little, we had carefully selected furniture and settled in to make a life in Anderson. She never did like clutter, and she loved simplicity. Our first home was made to look almost like a dollhouse with her incredible ability for decorating. She taught me to appreciate the beauty of keeping things simple, yet elegant. She wanted our home to be immaculate, but livable. Both of us were very frugal because of our upbringings, but we learned to make the most of what we had. Though we may not have understood it at the time, this was a principle we would value which would pay great dividends later in life.

The process of becoming one can be messy at times. Two people becoming one doesn't just happen. Even conflict can bring you closer together. Once, she created a real mess. As a southern boy, I enjoyed a bowl of cornbread and buttermilk. She, not so much. That day we had a slight argument about something, and I was sitting at the kitchen table with my bowl of cornbread and buttermilk. Something I said angered her immensely, and she walked over to slap the bowl out of my hand onto the floor, and the entire contents of my bowl flew up against the wall. We both had a good laugh. She made me clean it up. She convinced me her getting angry was my fault—and this wouldn't be the last time she did something like that. The treasure of married love is making up after you argue. As soon as possible, you must come back together. We both enjoyed the making up part. And that night, we found a way to do just that.

All progress in the Christian life comes first by experiencing the cross and then the resurrection. Talk about polar opposites—those two things are as different as night and day. Married love is like that as well—there is a cross to bear and there is a triumphant resurrection to be lived. All too often, marriages suffer wounds because of an inability to express love in times of conflict. Thankfully, Shirley and I were taught the principle of directing our anger toward the enemy attacking our marriage rather than at each other. True married love does not insist on its own rights, and it's never self-seeking, it's never selfish. True love gives and gives, and never just to get. Again, we learned that marriage requires four things: two givers and two forgivers. Love is not love because it suffers long; it is love because, in its suffering, it is kind. Every married couple should realize there are times (many times) when you must continually love each other even when you don't like your spouse's actions or words. The cross is a covenant that deals with our sins, and the resurrection is a covenant that gives us life. Both of these events were covenants of love given to us by God. Sometimes marriage is a cross to bear, but there should always be a resurrection to new life.

Not long after we were married, we discovered both of us were optimists. That simply means you look for and expect the very best outcome of anything—person or circumstance. Almost every spouse comes into a marriage with high expectations of what it will offer them. Sometimes the expectation is far greater than the reality. If you expect far more than what you eventually get, there will be great disappointment. We found that expectations should not be set in concrete. When your expectation level is a ten and your reality is a three, there is a huge disappointment gap. The solution is for each spouse to temper their expectation, thereby narrowing the gap. The narrower the gap, the better the marriage relationship. Expectation will often determine your perspective on something.

> **True covenant, married love has the supernatural power of self-recovery.**

Psychologists tell us we don't believe what we see, we see what we believe. Optimism has to do with how we see what we see. True love is not afraid to face life. The burden of life can't crush it.

True covenant, married love has the supernatural power of self-recovery.

What every couple needs to possess is boundless spiritual elasticity, giving each other the benefit of the doubt when possible. Love is capable of wonderful submission and often quietly accepts what life brings.

After that first year of marriage, with the Vietnam War raging, it appeared I would be drafted. Joining the National Guard, I spent the next six long years in the Army. They shipped me off to Fort Jackson, South Carolina, for eight weeks of basic training. Let me tell you—I hated being in the Army. I have nothing against the military, but I hated being away from Shirley, who at this time was seven months pregnant with our firstborn, Darin. Since Columbia was only an hour and a half drive, she came down to visit on the weekend, and then I would go home for a weekend. I wasn't always given a pass to go home, but I went home anyway. Sometimes you need to make executive decisions in life. At the end of basic training, I was assigned to Fort Lee, Virginia, and was even farther from my bride than I ever wanted to be. The next ten weeks were spent there before arriving back home in February—just in time for Darin to be born. (For the next six years, I had National Guard meetings one weekend a month.) Life was really good. Shirley, Darin, and I—on a pilgrimage, a journey, that would soon see several major changes. Wow, did God have other plans! The Army stint was a rude interruption in our very wonderful life. Knowing who you really are is your greatest asset—it will carry you through some stressful moments in life. While in the Army, those questions popped up in my mind again. Who am I? What am I? Why am I?

You can never become the person God created you to be until you get past your past. Anytime we don't know and understand our purpose, or who we were created to be, we become vulnerable to manipulation. God has an eternal seat reserved for us, a special one-of-a-kind seat with our names engraved on it. Sin, lies, rejection, abandonment, and absence have no power to keep you from becoming who God created you to be. When you discover your identity, you will live in truth. The Army taught me I am not a military person. Back home with the wife of my dreams, we continued our journey of married love. That would not be the last time those questions would arise in my thinking. Arriving there just in time for Darin's birth, we wanted to make up for the times of separation the Army had caused.

After Darin was born, I began working at the bank part-time, and I would travel some with Tony, who worked with American Home Foods as a sales rep. Living in a four-room house was going to get crowded if we wanted another baby, which we planned, so his uncle built us a larger house on 714 Cypress Lane. I wanted a wood beam ceiling, a fireplace in the den, and I had to have my living room—which, by the way, we never sat in. Since his uncle was building the home, we had our pick of lots. We chose a half-acre lot with trees, and there we lived for five years. How blessed can you be? We settled into our seven-room brick home and enjoyed three wonderful years as a family of three living the dream.

It was 1969, and Shirley was now pregnant with our daughter, Melony. Our family would be blessed with a son and a daughter, and a very wonderful life that was close to family and friends. All the while, I was unfulfilled and trying to come to grips with what that meant. Driving on my job as a sales rep, tears would flow down my face as I prayed, asking God for direction. Shirley was a loving, encouraging, supportive wife and a patient, understanding mother to our two children. Our marriage could not have been better, and our home life was filled with joy. During Melony's birth, Shirley's blood pressure rose to a dangerous level, and the doctor suggested we have no more children. There were no more issues after her birth, and our family of four seemed complete. During this time, I kept my feelings of uneasiness from Shirley since I didn't know what to tell her. Imagine the pain I was feeling inside knowing things were going to change. This beautiful treasure of married love God had blessed us with did not fulfill the deep desire to be used by Him. Valuable treasure is never discovered sitting on top of the ground—you must dig for it. What I did not understand at the time is the process God would use to get us there. He had allowed us to grow together for more than four years, creating a powerful spirit of oneness. People often say how it seemed that our marriage was one made in Heaven.

Here I was with a beautiful wife, two children, a promising career, a large home, and something was missing. When we look back now, we realize that God gave us over four years to build a solid foundation of love, affirmation, and acceptance in our relationship. These years would help us weather the storms brought on by the change which was about to occur.

Life was really good—two wonderful children, a beautiful home, good jobs, and a great church. Seemingly we had everything we wanted in life, but then God turned our world upside down. Our life story experienced a dramatic change one Saturday morning. It came on so suddenly, out of nowhere, and I was very unsuspecting of it. Tony has shared this story often on how this changed our lives.

One Wednesday evening, I was coming out of North Augusta, trying to get home in time for church—about a ninety-minute drive. That day, the rain was really coming down. I was alone in the hotel with a heavy burden, and often I laid on the floor and cried. Working my job during the day, then coming back to the hotel at night, I would pray and cry some more. God was dealing with my heart. When I headed home that night, I was crying. Praying and weeping as I was coming up the road, I could hardly see twenty feet in front of me because of the rain. Something inside of me wanted to get home and go to church. While praying I remember asking God to speak to me.

Suddenly, on the front of the hood, a form appeared. Whether or not it was an angel, I can't say. My tears stopped and a strange peace came over me. As a family, we went to church that night. Over the next few months, God began to show me His future for us. I was a very happy salesperson, had a company car to drive, had a brand-new house on a nice half-acre wooded lot. Shirley was working at the bank. We had a wonderful life and yet, God said, "That is not the one I have chosen for you." A beautiful hidden treasure was about to be discovered through an incident that happened at the end of a very frustrating week for me.

On Saturday morning, I took the children with me to the grocery store, so Tony could do some office work for his job. After driving up the street, I realized I had forgotten my purse. I returned to the house and pulled into the garage. When I tried to open the door, it was locked, which I thought was very strange because we didn't usually lock the door during the day. I rang the doorbell and when Tony finally came to the door crying, I asked him what was wrong.

He said, "I am miserable and cannot live like this. God is calling me into the ministry, but I don't feel adequate for the task."

This was all a surprise to me; he had never mentioned any of this. I thought to myself: How could he be a minister when he was so shy and timid? I called our pastor (Evan Landreth) and asked him to come over.

"What is wrong with you, Tony?" he asked.

Tony answered, "I am miserable. God called me into the ministry when I was 16, but I have been running from it ever since."

Pastor Landreth began to laugh and said, "Tony, there are a lot of things worse than preaching."

He stayed for a while, prayed with us, and from that day on, we knew that our lives would never be the same. Tony was always a very hard worker and during the next two years, he not only worked for American Home Foods but also sold and laid carpet for a friend of ours. Both of us knew we had to pay all our debts off, so Tony could go to Lee University and get a degree. Over the next two years, we would sometimes travel on weekends to preach at churches. People would often remark Tony didn't speak like he was just starting in ministry. (He once told me he promised God he would give every ounce of his life if God would restore the years that Tony ran from his calling.) Truly, God took him up on his commitment.

Often, we would hear about speakers, evangelists, holding meetings even in different states. Our travels to these various meetings were about Tony learning from great men of God-how to speak and conduct a service. In reality, God was setting up some of these moments to bring people into our lives who would pour into us, mentoring us for the cause of His Kingdom. God is always concerned about the details of where He is taking us. A real reason for being at the service that night was to hear T.L. Lowery who was currently serving as lead pastor of the Church of God in Cleveland, Tennessee. Later, he would become our pastor, mentor, and friend. Tony loved to hear Dr. T.L. Lowery speak because he was a great man of God who was accomplishing tremendous things for His Kingdom.

While attending a revival service in Buford, Georgia, we came to know Dr. Raymond Culpepper. Conversing with him after church, he mentioned he was selling his mobile home. We inquired as to his price and finally agreed to purchase it and made plans to move it to Cleveland, Tennessee. Neither of us liked the idea of going to Cleveland and renting a place, so meeting Dr. Culpepper and hearing him say, "I'm selling my mobile home" was simply a God appointment. It was practically new, and we got a good deal.

An important principle in the treasure of married love is the discovery that your life story is one of perpetual becoming. Shirley and I didn't realize it at the time, but God was putting together the pieces of our future life. God wanted us to learn to respond to life instead of just reacting. Jesus was a responder, and He never reacted. Identity is discovered at the core of your being, not on the surface, as you respond to the challenges of life.

Living in Anderson and enjoying our wonderful life, we never realized God had buried our true identities in the core of our beings. Actually, we were extremely confident in who we were, what we were doing, along with the beauty of being close to our families. An amazing discovery for us was coming to know from our deep inner-natures who we were and how that would affect every area of our life.

> The real you, your real life, is not measured by time—days, months, years—but by the thoughts that fill your mind and the purposes that truly engage your heart.

Only God can tell you who you really are—not circumstance, not people, not things. Our identity is intended to be built over the course of our life as we respond to the issues of our lives. Circumstance will often reveal who you are, but it should never determine who you are. The real you, your real life, is not measured by time—days, months, years—but by the thoughts that fill your mind and the purposes that truly engage your heart.

Shirley, Darin, Melony, and I were thoroughly enjoying our life. Our families lived at most an hour away from us. Every Sunday, we gathered at my mother's house where all of her children came bringing their favorite dish. Mom loved this more than anything. Although we had a great church to attend and many church friends to fellowship with, there always seemed to be something missing from our lives. While we didn't have many conversations about this issue, both of us had a sense there was more to life than what we were experiencing. God was about to permit circumstances that would create a spiritual hunger which could no longer be met in our local church.

Life and its issues demand, insist, that the way we think of and respond to God is the most practical thing we do. Knowing who you are in His Kingdom is the most critical issue in living a life of significance.

The Psalmist said, before God formed you in your mother's womb, He knew you and wrote a book about your life (Psalm 139).

This chapter in the Psalms caused me to want to know who He made me to be. Once again, those questions arose in my mind: Who am I really? What am I? Why am I?

Over the next two years, Shirley and I grew closer to God than ever before, and as a result, closer to one another. God was bringing us into oneness with Him and with each other. **One + One = One** was happening—it was forming. Even today as I think about how she acclimated herself in the transition to Kingdom ministry, I marvel at her wisdom and grace. Over the next several years, she and I would often have to dig deep to figure out where this would all lead. There was no place for shallow living now. We had to be all in and never look back. It is said the most valuable treasures are found in the deepest parts of the Earth. This is also true of our spiritual treasure—it can only be found at the core of our being. Shirley could have resisted these radical changes and transitions we were experiencing. Every day I thank God for the treasure she was, God's most valuable gift to me on this Earth. Through it all, she exuded strength, wisdom, compassion, love for God, for me, and the children until the day she left us—and that never changed.

Tony and I were about to experience a radical transformation in our lives. God had permitted us to have all that we could possibly want—our beautiful new home, our two children, and the deep abiding love we had for each other.

My dream of attending a great church and raising my children there was going to be challenged in ways that I couldn't have ever dreamed. Great disciplines would have to be learned in this transition. The treasure of true married love, which God had buried within us, would prove to be our anchor in the many years ahead.

Love is completely trusting, always eager to believe the best in each other. Love always sees the bright side of every situation without despair. In our flesh, we would have preferred our lives continue on the course we were on. God was bringing about a great dissatisfaction within, which only He could have permitted. True married love—God-style—endures amidst great challenge, transition, and even conflict. Tony and I would learn to endure the challenges of the weeks, months, and years ahead because of our love for God and our love for each other.

As we were about to begin a new chapter in our unfolding love story—our autobiography—our love and devotion to God and each other would only deepen. Interestingly, the word "biography" comes from two words that describe the human canvas of our lives: *graphim* (what is written) and *bios* (our living cells).

Daily, hourly, minute by minute, we were writing the story on the living cells of our life. God had prepared us over the last seven years of our marriage for the new journey we were on. As we learned to surrender to His uncaused and unconditional love for us, we began to experience great peace about our decision for Tony to attend Lee College.

Finally, in August 1972, Tony resigned from his position at American Home Foods, and I resigned from my position at the bank. We sold our home, our furniture, except for a few pieces, and relocated to Cleveland, Tennessee. Often, we would be aware God had made us so much one that our thoughts, though unspoken, would be known by the other. **One + One = One.**

Saying goodbye to our families was very emotional, and we pulled away with tears running down our faces. At that moment, we were extremely happy and excited about our adventure with God, yet deeply saddened to leave our families. Soon God would bring new people into our lives, and some of them became our friends of the heart for the rest of our lives.

Upon arriving in Cleveland, I went to the Church of God General Headquarters and applied for a secretarial position. Amazingly, I was hired that day in World Missions. The four of us drove around Cleveland as Tony searched for a job. Someone told him a man was looking for a school bus driver. It was getting late in the afternoon, but Tony would not give up. He tracked the man down and asked if the school bus driver position was still available.

The man asked, "How did you find me?"

To which Tony replied, "I kept asking questions and your name came up."

"How did you know I would be here?" he asked.

Fortunately, a friend told us where to find him and Tony was hired that day. Talk about a whirlwind of events. We sold our house, most of our furniture, left our jobs, moved to Cleveland, Tennessee, and before the sun went down that day, we were both employed. God was teaching us who we really were as we discovered our identities in Him.

> During our lifetimes, we consistently do two things— we leave, and we enter.

During our lifetimes, we consistently do two things—we leave, and we enter.

For example, we leave home to enter work and then leave work to enter home. How you leave often impacts how you enter. This would be a principle we would learn to live out over the next forty-six years of our life. In the process of living this principle, we determined our home would be a sanctuary. Whatever frustrations, challenges, and adversities life would bring us during the day, we would enter the comfort of our home and just be us. All too often, marriages experience strife because of the inability to abide by this principle.

Shakespeare once said, "Parting is such sweet sorrow."

Shakespeare once said, "Parting is such sweet sorrow."

That is truly what we experienced when we left Anderson, South Carolina and entered Cleveland, Tennessee. For this principle to work properly, we have to learn the treasure of discipline.

Oneisms from Chapter 2

- True love is not afraid to face life. The burden of life can't crush it.

- There is a cross to bear and there is a triumphant resurrection to be lived. True married love does not insist on its own rights and it's never self-seeking, it's never selfish. True love gives and gives, and never just to get.

- True covenant married love has the supernatural power of self-recovery. What every couple needs to possess is boundless spiritual elasticity.

- Sin, lies, rejection, abandonment, and absence have no power to keep you from becoming who God created you to be.

- An important principle in the treasure of married love is the discovery that your life story is one of perpetual becoming.

Chapter 3

The Treasure of Discipline

DISCIPLINE truly is the balance of life. While at Lee, God was transitioning us into our forever life which He pre-programmed into our DNA. Although we were always very disciplined, we were about to learn spiritual disciplines that would follow us for the rest of our days.

Nothing is more critical to successful, significant living than knowing who you are. The formation of our inner natures greatly affects the cultivation of our outward habits. We were about to be educated about these disciplines needed for a life of significance in His Kingdom.

When we discipline ourselves and our desires to live within the confines of His Word, according to the principles of His Word, it is then that we begin to experience God in His fullest measure. Those who are His church on Earth express the fullest, most complete thought of God concerning His Son Jesus. The disciplined life will bring a good life.

Self-examination is always important no matter what stage of life you are in.

- If you are not getting what you want out of life... then you need self-discipline.

Socrates once said, "The unexamined life is not worth living."

- If you feel like you're losing control...then you need self-discipline.
- If you find yourself surrendering the leadership of your life to runaway emotions and moods... then you need self-discipline.

Socrates once said, "The unexamined life is not worth living."

If you have a desire for a life of significance, if you want to get a handle on your moods to master them, and if you long to succeed where you have been failing, then you need to develop spiritual disciplines. With them, you can control your life, rather than your life controlling you. You can take charge of your life and become an achiever.

Very often, self-discipline is what we need most and want the least. Many people have a natural inclination to be lazy. There is within us a pull toward taking the path of least resistance. It is through self-discipline we bring out the best within us. It is a necessary exercise needed to fulfill a goal—a way to improve yourself. After all, you should strive to be the best possible version of yourself. Who did God mean when He meant me? Who is the real me? Until you go to the core of your being, you will never really understand yourself. In the New Testament, we learn that God chastises the ones He loves. The word "chastise" is actually the word "education," so God educates us as to our value, importance, and significance for His Kingdom. What you want out of life is to discover the God-life you were truly created for. We were about to learn that.

Until this point, our lives had been lived under the influence of outward things such as family, faith, friends, and occupation. Creating spiritual disciplines would take us where we had not been. God wanted us to dig deep to the frontier of our most intense desires, so He could reveal the calling written within our hearts. We were learning life is not a problem to be solved, but an adventure to be experienced. Somewhere in the world is a hunger your deepest desires will address. Unless you create spiritual disciplines, you'll never fully achieve the calling God has for your life. Spirit, soul, and body are created by God to be honed, sharpened by discipline.

From the beginning of our courtship and throughout our entire marriage, we understood the necessity of discipline. Every morning, we had a routine of getting up, making the bed, then getting ready to leave for work. Before we left, dishes had to be in the dishwasher, clothes picked up or put in the laundry basket; in essence, the house had to look neat and orderly. Shirley was always very organized and taught me to love it. I remember we owned some glass-topped tables. She always had the Windex in one hand and a paper towel in the other. I had placed a cup of coffee on one, and she didn't like the mess it left. She also had an incredible gift for organization. She hated clutter and would always put things back in place. Her uniqueness made me appreciate her even more. She was disciplined in ways I was not. The disciplines we were learning at these early stages of our marriage would later have a profound effect on our lives.

Before moving to Cleveland, both of us were volunteers at our church. We drove the bus to bring people to church services and worked to build up the Wednesday night service. Our pastor knew he could depend upon us to do whatever was needed. There was never a time when we just attended church—we were always contributing members.

Our transition to Cleveland, Tennessee, and Lee University was made easy because of how intensely we felt God's calling into ministry. We had known for some time that as good as our life was, we were finally experiencing the missing link. God had buried something inside of our spirit that was yearning to be released.

> Frederick Buechner said, "We are in constant danger of being not actors in the drama of our lives but reactors, to go where the world takes us, to drift with whatever current happens to be running the strongest."

Frederick Buechner said, "We are in constant danger of being not actors in the drama of our lives but reactors, to go where the world takes us, to drift with whatever current happens to be running the strongest."

Understanding the difference between acting out the God-story of our life, or just reacting to the events of our life proved to be a great treasure in our personal lives and ministry.

While attending Lee University, God brought very special people into our lives who made phenomenal deposits into us. Bill George was a colleague at General Headquarters where Shirley worked. He became a life-long friend and later helped me write the book, *The Diamond Life: You Are More Than You Have Become.* Dr. T.L. Lowery, our pastor, spiritual father, and mentor was responsible for assigning us to the church in Toledo. He greatly influenced our understanding of God's power and anointing.

With us both working full time (I was also going to school), Darin in school, and Melony in daycare, discipline was mandated. There are many things we learned during this season.

Your calling is discovered when your deepest desires and the hunger of the world meet. One's calling demands discipline to produce significance.

Two key principles for life in His Kingdom are: trust and obedience.

Your calling is discovered when your deepest desires and the hunger of the world meet. One's calling demands discipline to produce significance.

Two key principles for life in His Kingdom are: trust and obedience.

One Sunday after church, we came home knowing we didn't have the money to go out to eat as a family. We were actually picking up every couch cushion in hopes of finding any spare change that might be there, trying to scrounge up enough money to go to McDonald's or Krystal. A beautiful green Cadillac pulled up outside our mobile home, and there was Gail Gammill. Hershel, her husband, was a national evangelist, and we were beginning a great friendship with them which would last more than 40 years.

She came in and sat down on the couch and said, "After church today, the Lord impressed me to write a check to you, and I felt like I had to give it to you now."

We prayed over it, thanked her, and she left. When we looked at the check, it was for $25. It could have easily been $250 at that moment for us. To this day, we are thankful for Gail's obedience to God. There are so many of these stories that show the discipline of God's Kingdom in our lives. He was teaching us that when we live by Kingdom principles of trust and obedience, His blessings flow.

When I first arrived on campus and received my schedule of classes, I went over to the bookstore to purchase what I needed. Two days later, sitting in class, I noticed a young man did not have a book for the class. After the class, I asked him where his books were; he only had enough money to enroll, but not enough for the books. At that moment, God told me to buy his books. God was teaching me discipline—trust, obedience. We both went to the bookstore and I bought all his books that day. That night as we ate together, I told Shirley what happened. "We don't have a lot of money, but we need to be obedient when He speaks," she agreed.

One week later, I came home after my janitorial job at General Headquarters and stopped by the mailbox. Inside was a nice card, but I didn't recognize the address. After entering the mobile home, I opened the card. Aunt Lena, whom I had not seen in many years, said she was praying, and the Lord told her to send me a check. The amount was $100, four times what I paid for the young man's books. While we had practiced personal disciplines for several years, God was now teaching us spiritual disciplines.

Spiritual discipline is preparation for release. It is the road to greater freedom. It teaches us to become givers rather than takers. That leads to a lifestyle of generosity continually paying big dividends.

The whole world of achievement belongs to the person who will put forth the willpower to practice spiritual disciplines. Everyone who practices self-discipline of the body has more energy and zeal to press forward while others might wear out. The beginning of self-discipline is when you wake up to the fact there are undisciplined areas in your life, and you determine to do something about it. You have to remember there are no shortcuts. Great achievements come through great self-discipline. Positive self-discipline is giving whatever you're doing your best shot. Simply believe you can.

Growth and increase in life involve consciously cutting out anyone and anything that does not aid in reaching the goal you have set. It involves patiently building into your life those skills and habits of thought and action that make the goal reachable.

One of the great motivations for self-discipline is understanding why we're here. The answer from the Bible is that God intends to use you. He wants you. He made you. He designed you, with all the particular abilities you have and the unique talents and gifts He has given you, that you might be useful and pleasing to Him.

Getting into college and going to class, working two jobs, and speaking on the weekends was a very taxing lifestyle. We would often drive home on Sunday night, getting home in the wee hours of the morning to start another week. I didn't know anyone at Lee, and as I looked around, I saw the sons of many prominent men. That day I went home to pray and stopped to pick up Melony from the daycare center. I gave her some things to play with in her room.

I went back to my bedroom and cried out to God, "Lord, I don't have anyone to help me. I don't know anyone. No one knows who I am. How can I ever make it in the ministry?"

Those same questions came again: Who am I? What am I? Why am I?

I heard something fall to the floor and ran into Melony's room. She had pulled a photo album off the shelf, and the photos were spread everywhere on the floor.

"Melony Dawn Scott, who do you think you are?" I asked.

She replied, "I ain't nobody."

Tears flowed from my eyes. I had just said to God: "What can you do with me?"

Melony was teary-eyed, and I think she was saddened. We picked up the photos together, and she knew I wasn't mad at her.

A few days later, I was in the same back bedroom praying, thinking about Elisha with these very words: "Where is the God of Elijah?"

Later my mom called to speak with us—Shirley, the kids, me. I was on the phone with her last.

She said, "Son, I am very concerned about you."

"Why mom, why are you concerned?"

"While I was praying, I heard you say, 'Where is the God of Elijah?'"

I could hardly believe my ears. There I was telling God I was a nobody, and He showed me who He is and that He heard me. Things were now getting deep. My mom's phone call, actually knowing the words I had prayed, and the episode with Melony were a little beyond my spiritual understanding. That night, I shared the events which happened that day with Shirley. Both of us were astounded at God's love and attention for us, and His communication to us. And since He hears me, He knows me. God has so arranged our lives to work best when we live by faith. Daily, He is willing to help us write the script, the story of our lives. With God, there are no formulas for life. He just says, "In all of the things of your life, I will work for your good."

Mystery is essential for adventure. God's Kingdom is a mystery. Only by becoming one with Him can we obtain an understanding of that Kingdom.

Webster's defines discipline as "instruction; a branch of learning; training, or mode of life in accordance with rules; subjection to control; order maintained by control." It comes from a Latin word that means "disciple." His Kingdom is based on discipline and order, which operates with laws and rules. It is maintained by His control. God is deep; there is no searching for His understanding.

Very few shallow people ever exemplify the characteristics of discipline. To be a disciplined person requires depth.

What our world needs today is not a greater number of intelligent or gifted people, but many more deep people—people willing to move beyond surface living and into the deeper depths of life. From the beginning, God's message to man was about discipline.

In Genesis 2:15 (AMPC), He said, "...and the Lord God took the man and put him in the Garden of Eden to tend and guard and keep it." This is the very first principle given by God to man concerning discipline and self-control. In essence, man was to serve God in obedience to His command in order for his life to be disciplined. The two trees in the Garden constitute a great example of human discipline and its fruit. Eat of the Tree of Life, and you will live forever, but if you eat of the Tree of the Knowledge of Good and Evil, you will die. God is teaching Adam and us the principle of learning to be accountable for the responsibilities He has placed upon us to live a disciplined life.

Accountability for responsibility.

Shirley was far more disciplined than me. When something needed to be done, she would just do it. She never put off until tomorrow what she could do today. Even with all the responsibilities of a growing family, both of us working, and me being in school, we took the time to meet each other's needs. Our love for each other was always so strong that we never wanted to be apart even for a day or night. Occasionally, we would do lunch and just spend that time alone with each other. The more we experienced oneness with God, the more we wanted to be one with each other.

Accountability for responsibility.

The treasure of true love—the kind God has for us—is the only foundation on which to build a marriage. Never did I think of Shirley as my possession. My love for her was based on her value, her worth. How could I help her to realize her full potential as a woman? She loved me in the same way. To know her love was the greatest treasure God ever let me experience. We were each fulfilled by that unconditional love. She did not have to perform to receive it from me, nor did I have to perform to receive it from her. I didn't love her out of need—I needed her because I loved her. **One + One = One!**

College life proved to be very hectic. With both of us working and then traveling and speaking on weekends, sometimes the kids would complain because of the long car rides. Often, we would head out on Friday afternoon and then drive back late Sunday night. Little did we know this was minor stress compared to the stress of pastoring a church which we would later experience, yet we always wanted to focus on quality family time. Thankfully, we had some great mentors. Gay and Floyd Lawhon, Hershel and Gail Gammill, Bob and Judy Blackaby—all of these couples and families we met during our time in Cleveland. Having experienced a great amount of success in ministry, we benefited greatly from their wisdom and knowledge of ministry life and what it requires. Tony had always been timid and shy about meeting new people—he always pushed me forward to make the connections. God had blessed me with such a love for people that it was always easy to meet and to make new friends.

At Lee University, there was a Ministers' Club on campus to which Tony belonged. Off-campus, there was a Ministers' Wives Club which I became a part of. In our second year, I was elected president of this club. Mildred Lowery was one of the sponsors, and it allowed Tony and me to develop a lifelong relationship with Dr. T.L. Lowery and his wife. Being elected president was quite a surprise, but Tony was always proud of my accomplishments. Sometimes I wondered if he was a little intimidated because it was so easy for me to meet people while at the same time it was somewhat of a challenge for him. Being at Lee helped us to develop strong relationships with ministers and their wives, which we would enjoy throughout the years. Though our closest friends were those who were a little older than us, Tony and I were older than many of the younger couples. By the time we arrived at Lee, we had been married for seven years and had two children. Many times, we were able to help the younger couples who perhaps had only been married for two or three years and were experiencing the stresses of college life and ministry. The fact that we were one and we were in this together were our biggest strengths. Our love for each other was very passionate, and we were best friends. God helped me to understand how much Tony needed my support. In some things, we were

> Be in the same book, in the same chapter, on the same page, in the same paragraph, in the same sentence, and on the same word. Oneness.

totally opposite (and that's okay because God made us different), but we were always one. We learned to celebrate our differences rather than let them be contentious.

Be in the same book, in the same chapter, on the same page, in the same paragraph, in the same sentence, and on the same word. Oneness.

This was something Tony taught me that greatly increased our sense of oneness.

I always wanted him to look good no matter what he was involved in. And he was always so proud of anything that I accomplished. His unselfish love and devotion to me were always on display. Throughout our years together, I was constantly aware of that love. Looking back, I know we did not have some of the challenges young married couples sometimes have in their relationships because we always knew God brought us together. As we intermingled with other young couples, even before going to Lee, it was obvious something special was going on with us which was sometimes missing from their lives. Seems like we ended up counseling others a lot even before we accepted our ministry role. There was a depth to our relationship which we probably took for granted, but others often noticed. **One + One = One** is a powerful mandate of God for every married couple.

Divorce was never a topic of discussion for us even when life was challenging and difficult. Because we worked together as a team, we really didn't experience financial pressures as some did. Watching a couple that we knew who ended up getting a divorce was beyond our ability to comprehend. You will hear me say this over and over... our love story was one for the ages. We felt our love story was truly a match made in Heaven. Tony and I experienced this kind of love because God chose us each for the other. Now I would not have you to be ignorant—there were challenges! You have two Type-A personalities who also both possess stubbornness—he more than me. But the joy of those times would be when we would make up, and we always made up! (Need I say more?) We learned early on that intimacy in marriage—sex—is very important for the bonding that God has provided for spirit, soul, body.

Never focus on what you don't agree with each other on; focus on that which brings you together.

Never focus on what you don't agree with each other on; focus on that which brings you together.

Our home church pastor was appointed as overseer of Arkansas. He had invited Dr. Lowery (our pastor) to be the main night speaker for the annual camp meeting in the summer of '73. Tony was invited to come with him and speak at one of the morning services.

I always wanted Tony to look good—nice clothes, shoes, to be the best he could be. In downtown Cleveland, there was a bargain basement store that sold clothes and shoes at discounted prices. There I found a pair of black lace-up dress shoes on sale for ten dollars. Though not in his size, I would stuff tissues in the toes to make them fit.

Tony was reluctant, but I convinced him it would work just fine. This was a great opportunity for him to speak in front of a large crowd—especially a statewide meeting. He tied the shoes as tight as possible, but they were still somewhat loose when he went to speak that morning. He was never one to stand still while he was speaking, and as he moved around, one shoe came off. He reached down and pulled it back on and continued to speak. It was about to come off again, so he turned to the back of the stage and flipped the shoe into the back curtain, slipped the other off, and put that one under the speaker stand while making a joke of it for the audience. The old saying of "If the shoe fits" just didn't fit here. He walked in front of the podium, now in his socks, and his heel sank into a microphone jack which drew electricity and caused him to jump several feet in the air. The people in the crowd got very excited thinking that surely God was moving!

Later, back in the room, he told Dr. Lowery what had happened. He laughed so hard, he rolled off the bed onto the floor. When he called to tell me what happened, we both had a laugh, and I'm quite sure he never wore those shoes again.

In June 1974, I graduated with a B.A. in Biblical Education from Lee University. Shirley's mom and dad, and my mother and sisters were there. Dr. Ray Hughes was also in attendance as a former president of Lee, and Shirley wanted me to take a picture with him. She was always so bold, and I envied that boldness. He knew Shirley because she worked at General Headquarters. He was the most prominent leader in our denomination at that time. He agreed and she took the picture. She was always thinking about me—always making the right connections, always wanting me to succeed.

Life after Lee was going to change dramatically, and within two short months we would be relocating to Toledo, Ohio. Neither of us could have possibly known the blessing and the challenges that awaited us. Slowly but surely, we were moving toward our purpose.

From the beginning of our marriage, we were determined to experience the oneness God promised to Adam and Eve in the Garden. Without oneness in the days ahead, the very pressures of being in ministry, raising a family, with a continuously growing church would have been too great. Very few couples ever come to the place of experiencing total oneness—spirit, soul, body. God had miraculously helped us to experience what I believe is the most mysterious principle of relationships in the Universe—oneness. As you will see, this principle positively affects relationships wherever they are— marriage, family, friendship, business, education. With this principle, relationships experience unlimited bonding and cooperation.

Oneisms from Chapter 3

- When we discipline ourselves and our desires to live within the confines of His Word, according to the principles of His Word, it is then that we begin to experience God in His fullest measure.

- Understanding the difference between acting out the God-story of our life, or just reacting to the events of our life proved to be a great treasure in our personal lives and in ministry.

- Spiritual discipline is preparation for release.

- Growth and increase in life involve consciously cutting out anyone and anything that does not aid in reaching the goal you have set. It involves patiently building into your life those skills and habits of thought and action that make the goal reachable.

- What our world needs today is not a greater number of intelligent or gifted people, but many more deep people—people willing to move beyond surface living and into the deeper depths of life.

Part 2:

Mystery of Oneness

Chapter 4

Living as One

OUR journey to this point was like a comedy and a tragedy. At the General Assembly in August, I was asked if I was interested in pastoring a church in Sylvania, Ohio, a small suburb of Toledo. In June, I had been invited to speak at this church for a series of meetings. The week before this I was in Macclenny, Florida and had experienced a great move of God, and the meetings were extended for another three days through Wednesday night. A high school teacher, bringing many of her students with her, came to the meeting and received Christ. The church was packed. Leaving there, I traveled to Cleveland to spend three days with my family before arriving in Sylvania, Ohio on Saturday.

By the middle of the week, I called Shirley to tell her I was struggling because this church was dead. Having left Florida on a huge high with altars filled each night, I was now in Sylvania, and it felt like it was Ezekiel's dry bones that I was speaking to. Shirley encouraged me and was praying that God would move powerfully. By the weekend, we did have somewhat of a breakthrough, and God was indeed moving by His Spirit among the people. So when I was asked about coming there to pastor by Raymond Crowley, I did not know what to say. Shirley was at a ladies' meeting at the General Assembly and came to the room in the afternoon. I told her what had happened, and she and I prayed together about this opportunity. She asked how

I felt, and I remember saying: it's a great opportunity, but it's a long way from home. She reminded me of the promise we made to God, and we would go where He led us. After meeting with Dr. Crowley for breakfast the next morning, I agreed to make this move. We only had a short period of time to go back to Cleveland, sell our mobile home, pack up our furnishings, and move 650 miles. I was driving the U-Haul, pulling the Volkswagen behind, and she was driving the other vehicle. As you come upon the hill south of Cincinnati, there is a moment when it looks like you can only see infinity, and I was thinking, *My God, we have come to the end of the world.* Little did we know the challenge awaiting us when we arrived at the Holiday Inn on the south side of town. Because the pastor had not left the house provided by the church, we had to spend a couple of days there. When the phone rang in the room, I answered, and the state overseer was on the line. He expressed concern about my appointment since he was the new incoming state overseer. Nothing I learned in college prepared me for what I was about to experience in my first pastorate.

I remember his words to this day: "That is a very challenging church—you will be the fifth pastor in six years, and I'm not sure if you can handle it. So I have arranged for you to go to Washington, Pennsylvania, and pastor a church there."

I said, "Sir, God sent me to Toledo, and I don't think I'll be going to Washington, Pennsylvania."

"You will need to obey those who have the rule over you in the Lord," he said.

"Besides that, have you ever thought something was God's will and then found out it wasn't?" Being unfamiliar with protocols in the hierarchical system of government in the Church of God, I made the mistake of bringing up Dr. Lowery's name (who was on our executive committee at the time).

He said, "Well, Dr. Lowery is not the overseer of northern Ohio, I am."

I said, "I suggest you call him."

"I'll let him know," he assured me.

After hanging up, I called Dr. Lowery and informed him of this conversation.

He said, "Tony, do you believe that God wants you to pastor that church?"

I said, "I definitely do. Shirley and I both feel strongly about it."

He said, "Stay right where you are, and I will handle this."

A short time later, the overseer called to let me know he had spoken with Dr. Lowery.

"Well, Tony, it looks like they made the appointment, but you will have to stay in touch and talk to me every Sunday night to let me know how things are going."

In no uncertain terms, he let me know that he was unhappy with this situation.

It was early in the afternoon on Wednesday; I was to speak for the first time that night with this trauma on my shoulders. Often when we traveled together, Shirley would entertain the kids while I went into the bathroom to pray on the occasions we were in a hotel. Later that afternoon, I called the pastor so I could meet him and get the keys and prepare for that night.

He said, "I think I'll stay, so I can introduce you."

I let him know that wouldn't be necessary, and I would take care of everything else. So there we were. I was the appointed pastor of a church. It was Wednesday night—29 people and our family— God truly moved that night, and we knew that we were where He wanted us.

I remember our first service like it was yesterday. It was a Wednesday night, and God spoke to us, assuring us that He would be with us to lead and guide the church to a place of breakthrough. We were so encouraged that we began to work hard contacting everyone who had ever attended the church. We invited them back and encouraged them to bring their families and friends to be part of the movement of God.

While I did not forget the overseer's request to speak with him every Sunday night, I decided to wait until the end of the month. Each week, I would encourage the congregation to invite family and friends. Each week, we would increase in attendance. The mortgage payment was behind several months, and the interest rate was raised. By the end of the first month, our attendance had grown to 150—all past due bills had been paid, and I went to the bank to demand the interest rate be lowered to the original rate. It wasn't a pleasant meeting, but they agreed. The last night of September, we set an all-time high tithe, offering, and attendance record. I called the overseer at midnight. When he answered, it was apparent he had been asleep.

"You asked me to call you with our progress. I have been so busy with the rapid growth of the church that I have not had time."

"What's wrong?" he asked.

I replied, "There isn't anything wrong, but many things right. Attendance has increased—bills have been caught up, including the mortgage, and we have money in the bank."

"That's just one month; I wouldn't get too excited."

Then and there, I decided that was my last call to him to give our progress report. But over the next several months, he became a great friend. His three children often drove to the church on Saturday night from Akron, Ohio, for our services on Sunday. Over the ensuing months, our relationship grew, and he was much appreciative of the work being done.

Although I was raised in a pastor's home and was very involved in church work, nothing prepared me to be a pastor's wife. God knew in my heart I wanted to be in a local church and have a normal life that did not include ministry. Once Tony and I were sure of his calling into ministry, both of us gave it everything we had. He was always the visionary, and I was the detail person—the organizational person. Tony was so excited about all the new people coming to the church he decided to ask Dr. Lowery to come to speak in November. He had been our pastor for two years in Cleveland and was continuing to mentor us. Dr. Lowery was a powerful minister and greatly used by God. The church was filled to capacity and then some. He spoke Friday through Sunday night and raised the spiritual tide in the church. On Sunday night, God gave a prophetic Word through him:

"Behold I have set before you an open door, and no man can close it."

That Word came to pass and is still to this day happening in theChurch. God was beginning a mighty work of unity and oneness in a church where division and disunity had reigned. Many of the people began to gather around the vision as Tony ministered God's Word each week. He always believed in the principle which says,

Where God guides, He provides.

Certainly, that has proven to be true for us during all these years.

Our first revival started with a group of spiritually hungry young people. We invited them to our house on Thursday nights and sat on the floor talking about God's Presence and power in their lives. Maybe they came at first for the pizza, but God brought us into a oneness of spirit which truly ignited the church. Starting with only a dozen or so teenagers, soon there were more than 60. The first six rows of seats on the left side of the auditorium were filled each service with these firebrands as they hungered and thirsted for God. One of the great oneness principles of the Bible is found in Deuteronomy 32:30 (NIV): "How could one have chased a thousand, and two put ten thousand to flight, except their Rock had sold them, and the Lord had delivered them up?" Great miracles happened right before our eyes. A woman named Ruby fell and broke a bone in her wrist. She went to the emergency room and the x-ray showed a clean break. Since it was on Sunday, they applied a soft cast and told her to return on Monday when a surgeon would be available. At the Sunday night service, our group of young firebrands prayed over her asking God to heal the bone. When she returned to the hospital on Monday without the cast, they did another x-ray and saw no break. On Wednesday night at church, those same young people were ecstatic about the miracle. They experienced how powerful the Law of Oneness is in God's Kingdom. During the next few months, the church more than doubled in attendance as many people came to Christ. Today that youth group has moved across the country to different towns and cities with more than a dozen of them in either full-time or part-time ministry. On many occasions, pastors of churches where these young men and women would attend called me to share how they were so mature in their faith. Several of them remain in contact with us and with each other. "Oneness" drew them close to each other and close to God, and it has continued to influence their lives. A miracle changed their lives forever. Quite a number of them met their spouses in that youth group, and Tony performed their ceremonies—all of them are still married to this day. **One + One = One.**

Two people can never experience oneness in marriage until they learn to accept and appreciate their differences. It is one thing to be different and quite something else to teach your mate the value of those differences. Men feel just as deeply as women but don't express their emotions as easily as women do. All of us as human beings have two basic needs: security and significance. All of us want to be loved, accepted, and affirmed. Security is an awareness of being unconditionally, completely, wholly loved. Significance is the realization that I am valuable, and my life is worthwhile. I was always secure in Tony's love, and I knew he was secure in my love. Slowly but surely, I began to realize my value to him as a pastor's wife. God's remedy for these needs is an intimate, personal relationship with Him through His Son Jesus Christ. Both of us learned very quickly that our significance, self-worth, and self-esteem have to find their source in God.

From the beginning, we tried to love people, affirm them, and accept them for who they are. Discovering my purpose in life was the single greatest blessing I have ever received. God had given me the best mate, someone I loved with all my heart, and I wanted him to be the best he could be always.

During those first few years, we discovered that people carry a lot of hurt from their past. As the church was growing, a few people resisted the growth because of control issues. Until we arrived, the church was very small, and now it was beginning to grow. After the first year, there was a little bit of an uprising among three of the families. Tony was a strong leader and carried a heavy anointing of the Holy Spirit. Always very bold, he never really feared the attacks of the enemy. What he always needed was a filter, and I tried to be that for him. What I needed from Tony was for him to be the spiritual head of our house and know the mind of God for our family, not just the spiritual head of the church.

This trial drove us to our knees and to a oneness in God that we had never before experienced. There was much prayer, fasting, and many many tears. As Tony suffered from the stinging words of those who disagreed with the rapid growth of the church, we drew closer to God and closer to each other. More and more we were understanding the necessity of oneness with God and oneness with each other.

Without going into too many details, he eventually had to deal with these three families, and they all left the church. That very next week, we had an increase. And in February of 1975, Perry Stone came for a revival. More than 75 new people came into the church and multitudes were born again. Perry and Tony were the dynamic duo—both greatly anointed by God and used for His glory. That began a lifelong relationship, causing them to be as close as brothers. As the church continued to grow, there was a need for a new building—a gymnasium, a classroom facility that would house the Accelerated Christian School.

During this time, Tony would often work more than 70 hours per week. Trying to balance our family life with church life became very challenging. We had not learned the idea of "The main thing is to keep the main thing the main thing." One spring, Darin came up from the basement of our home, and he had tears in his eyes. I asked him what was wrong.

"Baseball is starting soon, and I wanted to play on a team, but Dad only has time for the church."

I went down to the basement where Tony was studying and praying, and we had a strong conversation about being a father as well as a pastor. He agreed with me, got his baseball glove, and went outside with Darin to throw the ball. Sometimes I felt his devotion to the church and love for the ministry were the biggest things in his life. During those years, we had difficult discussions and did not always agree on the time he was spending doing the work of God's Kingdom. For a season, our marriage was not what either of us wanted it to be—even though there was no question of our love and devotion for each other. It was then we learned a great principle of marriage—each of us had to be a giver and forgiver. Literally, we needed to learn how to have an argument—to agree to disagree all the while trying to maintain oneness in our relationship. Oneness in marriage is not just a biblical principle—it is the foundation of a true covenant marriage. Let me share with you some simple rules for achieving this **One + One = One** principle:

1. Value your spouse as God's gift to you.
2. Love each other unselfishly.
3. You should know what your spouse needs from you.
4. When conflict occurs, be willing to give up your right to be right.
5. Never go to sleep angry with each other.
6. Never resurrect settled conflict.
7. Be each other's cheerleader and encourager.
8. Make love often.

Since the home is the place where children learn the most about God, we need to take time to teach them His Word. An easy way to do this is around the dinner table. Instead of a prayer, have your child say a Bible verse. Try giving your child a Scripture verse to learn each week and then have him repeat it at dinner or when he says his prayers at night. There could be no better compliment than for your child, when he is grown, to say, "My parents taught me this verse around the dinner table."

I am so thankful to God we learned this principle and applied it to raising our children. I want to share with you some "divine order" principles God showed us in His Word, which we have put to practice in our oneness relationship. As we look back on their lives, we know God gave us many opportunities to be a part of their lives and encourage them to follow the dream God placed in their hearts.

Through searching the Scriptures, we set up a guideline for what we believed God's priorities were in the first family in Genesis:

First, God in our hearts and lives

Secondly, our relationship with our spouse

Thirdly, our relationship with our children

Fourthly, worshipping Him in Spirit and in Truth

Fifthly, our occupations in making a life

So often, wives compare their husbands to the perfect characters portrayed in movies and television, or the gentleman we see getting the door for his wife at church every weekend. What our comparisons don't consider is that actors have scriptwriters, and seemingly "perfect couples" are not that way all the time.

The key to having a more "perfect husband" is to be a more supportive wife. We need to realize men need respect, space, acceptance, and appreciation. Respect for your husband starts with refusing to compare him to other men, fictional or otherwise. Support him when he's facing a personal challenge and point out the things he does well when he's feeling defeated.

Often when a man is anxious, he may need some space. During those times, men will head to their man cave, literally or figuratively. Talking about it is not the thing they want to do and yet, that is exactly what I wanted to do. Through the years, I learned to let Tony have his space during those times while trying to pick a time to talk about it. Flexibility in relationships, especially with things you disagree about, is a wise standard to live by. Tony and I didn't always see eye-to-eye on things, but we learned to be flexible with each other's feelings. We came to understand oneness enhances every area of our lives—spirit, soul, body. All too often, God's statement to Adam and Eve—the two shall become one flesh—has only a physical, sexual connotation for those who read it. However, in the original language of the Old Testament, there is no question that God wanted us to be one in spirit, soul, body—in that order. When you truly seek to be one with your spouse, there is a synergy that develops which is both rewarding and energizing. Oneness is a process that is supposed to last throughout your entire married life.

Husbands need a little verbal applause and some honest adoration from time to time. Sincerely praise his efforts and attitudes. Every man needs a safe harbor where he can retreat, knowing he will be loved and appreciated. First and foremost, Tony desired my love and respect. My approval was always important to him.

Women who want to be treated like queens need to treat their husbands like kings. Instead of wishing for the "perfect man," start appreciating the one you have right now. The payoff will be a loving, lasting marriage of intimacy and security.

By making God's divine order a priority in our lives, we've seen our children mature in the Lord and our marriage grow stronger over the years. Establish God's priorities in your home today and begin ministering to your family. God is teaching me how to live my purpose and support my husband as Tony lives out his. Marriage is life on the fly with adjustments and transitions that bring about a process of order. God never wants marriage partners to compete with each other but to complete one another.

Unique, special, distinctive, rare, unequaled, matchless—that is how each of us can be described. Truly there is no one like each one of us—we are indeed one-of-a-kind. God designed marriage to bring us into oneness, where we are no longer two but now one. We become a team together, and we begin to understand oneness.

Oneisms from Chapter 4

- ❤ Be a giver and a forgiver.
- ❤ Establish God's priorities in your home today and begin ministering to your family.
- ❤ Oneness is a process that is to last throughout your entire married life.
- ❤ Love people, affirm them, and accept them for who they are.
- ❤ Where God guides, He provides.
- ❤ Learn to appreciate and accept the differences between you and your spouse in order to obtain oneness.
- ❤ Learn to keep the main thing the main thing.
- ❤ Sometimes in marriage, you have to agree to disagree.

Chapter 5

Law of Oneness

EVERY married couple should grasp these four concepts about the Law of Oneness:

1. It is a process. (It never ends.)

2. It is costly. (Selfishness not allowed.)

3. It is challenging. (Prepare to be stretched.)

4. It requires great determination. (Focus, focus, focus.)

Before you can ever experience true oneness in your marriage relationship, you must become one with Him and His purpose for you. Success in marriage is more than just finding the right person— it is more about being the right person. A "oneness marriage" is created by a husband and wife who continuously develop intimacy, love, trust, and understanding of one another. Adam and Eve were one with God and one with each other. To be "one" means to complement each other, to be one in purpose, passion, and vision.

God's design for spiritual and marital oneness requires four fundamental guidelines:

1. Severance (leaving)
    - Leaving all others

2. Permanence (cleaving)
    - Cleaving to each other

3. Unity (weaving)
    - Weaving your lives together

4. Intimacy (seeing)
    - Seeing into each other

To face the challenges of life daily, we need to leave a life of sin. We must continuously cleave to the promises of God's Word and the power of His Holy Spirit. We then weave our lives into the plans and purposes of God. "Spiritual nakedness" helps us approach His Throne holding nothing back, covering nothing up. Significance in life and His Kingdom come as we are one with His purposes. It equips us to face our challenges with courage and boldness.

One day as I studied Paul's words, they seemed to leap off the page into my heart—"the unity of the Spirit in the bond of peace" (Ephesians 4:3 KJV). God is always calling us to adjust our lives to His purposes. His purpose for us always perfectly aligns with His Kingdom business. God has uniquely gifted each of us and specifically designed our purpose to accomplish His Kingdom will. One passage that has often ministered to us and kept us while we were going through some difficult places is:

"For we are His workmanship [His own masterwork, a work of art], created in Christ Jesus [reborn from above—spiritually transformed, renewed, ready to be used] for good works, which God prepared [for us] beforehand [taking paths which He set], so that we would walk in them [living the good life which He prearranged and made ready for us]" (Ephesians 2:10).

God created us as a work of art—the putting of mind into matter, the action of thought upon stuff, the production of order out of chaos. God, the eternal artist, is creating His beauty from within us, expressing His divine nature through us, helping us to think His thoughts, and making poetic music out of our lives. He has done everything to ensure our complete and total success in His Kingdom purpose for us as we lean on Him. God never just sees us for who we are in our present circumstances, but who we can become as we fully surrender our lives to Him. This transformation is not possible without total surrender. Each of us is given the opportunity to discover and to live our purpose. At any given time, your challenges are permitted by God to reveal the reason for your birth. Daily, I must remind myself that I am God's poem, I am His workmanship, and I am His artwork. And... He is still working on me (and you)!

Shirley and I often were frustrated in our lives when we could not see the reason for our challenges. We gained strength from the story of Joseph. God never told him how he would become a great leader, but He designed and permitted challenges to cause Joseph to discover his purpose. Into our lives, He will allow circumstances, conflicts, and difficulties to adjust and mold us to fit the portrait He had of us before we were ever born.

O Lord, you have searched me [thoroughly] and have known me. You know when I sit down and when I rise up [my entire life, everything I do]; you understand my thoughts from afar. You scrutinize my path and my lying down, and You are intimately acquainted with all my ways. Even before there is a word on my tongue [still unspoken], behold, O Lord, You know it all. You have enclosed me behind and before, and [You have] placed Your hand upon me. Such [infinite] knowledge is too wonderful for me; it is too high [above me], I cannot reach it (Psalm 139).

Amazingly, He develops our character, His divine nature, within us as we experience rejection, pitfalls, isolation, and loneliness. It seems to me He never uses beautiful ingredients to form His image within us—usually, God takes the ugly, the bad, the bitter,

When you put a limit on who you can be, you put a limit on who you will be.

the difficult, the pain, and the suffering and makes something beautiful and valuable of our lives.

Life is always trying to limit us, to hinder us, to prevent us from becoming who we really are. God is always seeking to unshackle us, break the chains off us, to free us, and bring us into a relationship of oneness with Him which fulfills us. The Law of Oneness brings an exciting principle of life: Life without limits!

When you put a limit on who you can be, you put a limit on who you will be.

Someone once said, "When your dream becomes a vision, and your vision becomes your mission, you then live a life of purpose."

Your fulfillment in life is dependent upon you becoming who you were born to be and doing what you were born to do. In the depths of your being, there is a cry that never goes away— I want to live, I want to come alive, I want to live my highest life. There is a purpose for why we exist. Until that purpose is discovered and lived, you can never be fulfilled. Someone once said, "When your dream becomes a vision, and your vision becomes your mission, you then live a life of purpose."

It is possible to live a "filled" life and yet not be "fulfilled." Until you become one with your purpose, you can never be fulfilled.

Busyness in life does not always equate to production. Many times, couples are too busy living life to focus on the purpose of their relationship—becoming one. Earning a living is important, raising children is a major task, but all too often attention to the marriage ends up in last place. Intimacy was designed by God to bring a husband and wife close, to produce oneness, to fulfill each other's sexual desires. However, intimacy is more than sex. You could break the word down as follows: into—me—see. True oneness is accomplished in marriage when a couple experiences "soul nakedness."

Perhaps everyone knows nakedness means "without clothes." "Soul nakedness" is when you unwrap the innermost part of your being and invite your spouse inside your soul. In the depth of your being are thoughts that you may never share with another living soul—literally, you will go to your grave with them. However, some of those thoughts need to be shared. In order for your marriage to have depth, you must understand intimacy. Most men have a different idea of intimacy than women. Every man must understand there is a difference between intimacy and sex. For a woman, intimacy is more emotional than physical.

One of God's greatest gifts to us is coming to understand we each have different needs. We must ask ourselves the following question: What does my spouse need from me? From the very beginning, the stated purpose of a man and woman coming together as husband and wife was to experience oneness—in spirit, soul, body. For sure that doesn't happen just because a minister at your wedding says, "You are now one flesh." When God joined Adam and Eve together, they were naked and unashamed. Their nakedness extended to spirit and soul as well as body. Adam perfectly knew Eve; Eve perfectly knew Adam. The two of them perfectly knew God, and God perfectly knew them. To engage in the process of oneness is the highest expression of your married love: **One + One = One**.

Security in the marriage relationship is of the utmost importance to both spouses. A woman's greatest psychological need in marriage is to feel secure in her husband's love. My belief is it plays both ways. When God took a piece of Himself, His divine nature, and placed it within each human soul, we became capable of loving and being loved. Simply put, God is love. In your Christian experience, being secure in God's love is a sign of true maturity. Mature love is secure love. Likewise, in a marriage relationship, we long to feel secure in the way we are loved, thus affecting the way we love. Shirley never lived a day when she was not convinced of my love for her. (Of course, there were a couple of times when she wanted to kill me!) I also did not live one day when I was not convinced of her love for me. In dealing with my grief of her passing, I finally understand the greatest challenge of it. Sure, I miss her—her presence, the relationship we shared, the life we enjoyed. However, the greatest cause of my grief is the loss of her expressed love. The fact that she was willing to love me in spite of me was a treasure, a blessing I have no words to describe. When someone is loved unconditionally (mirroring Jesus), that love brings a powerful motivating, energizing force that anchors one's soul.

Always remember, God's love for us is unconditional, and it is also perfect. Nothing you can ever do will make Him love you more, nothing you will ever do will make Him love you less. When a marriage experiences the Jesus kind of love—when one learns to love their spouse as Jesus loves them—the power of love is exponentially multiplied. As you love God with your entire being—spirit, soul, body—and surrender gifts, talents, and abilities to His Kingdom use, you are loving Him as He loves you. He gave His all for you, to qualify you to give your all for Him. Far too often, spouses perform for love.

Love does not produce anxiety, it cures it. Love does not injure, it heals. Love does not diminish, it increases.

Sex is sometimes used as a reward in marriage, which in effect cheapens the very idea of it. Intimacy, along with a sexual relationship, was created by God so that each spouse could give their entire being to the other without reservation and without shame. Within every human being, there is a desire to love and be loved. Since God alone, by His Spirit, sows the seed of love into our lives, we must also sow that seed of love into our spouse.

Love does not produce anxiety, it cures it. Love does not injure, it heals. Love does not diminish, it increases.

Fulfilled love, which Shirley and I enjoyed with each other, is the God-kind of love. Interestingly, the Bible never gives a direct command to the wife to love her husband. A husband is directly commanded to love his wife. The reason is profound—as the priest of his home, he must become one with God in prayer and worship. Out of that experience, he is to love his wife. She will then amplify that love back to him, to the children, and to others. In the grind of day-to-day living, we become task-oriented. We miss the fact marriage is not a task; it's a living love relationship. The purpose of the marriage covenant is a loving, intimate, sexual relationship in which you give all of yourself to your spouse. You must never lose sight of this.

At one time in our marriage, I attempted to settle some conflicts by just praying about them. Soon I learned that prayer alone, without personal action on my part, was not sufficient. Shirley could definitely tell you I was not the most perfect spouse, and perhaps you may feel the same way at times in your relationship. That had little to do with my love for her.

Perhaps a real-life story will illustrate this better:

With a growing church staff, I thought it would be good to pull them away from the church for a retreat. At the time, there were six men and three women on staff. To bond with the men, I thought it best to have the first four-hour session with them. There was only one problem—I forgot to tell Shirley about this. When she found out, she was not a happy camper and let me know it. It had been a long time since I had seen her that angry. Later, I would learn she felt left out and dismissed, along with the other women, in this planning session. We met throughout that afternoon, and they were to join us for the evening meal. When she came in that night, the look on her face told me she was not over it. (Every woman has "the look"!) After the night session ended and we headed back to our home, I knew something had to be done. On the way home, God spoke to my heart and said, "You are the priest of your home, and you should fix this."

When we arrived home, I apologized and asked her to forgive me for being so insensitive to her needs as well as to the other women on staff. As always, she forgave me. The next day, we had a great session with all the staff. (I can assure you I never made that mistake again.) But it taught me a very valuable principle:

**Never approach conflict from
the standpoint of wanting to win—
approach it from the standpoint of love.**

There is a huge difference. God instructed me to approach her as the priest of our home and heal the breach. That's responding in love rather than trying to defend my position. This is where many people get into trouble in their marriages. It's not about defending your turf; it's about showing your love during conflict and remembering you love each other.

Being raised in a home with very little love between my mom and dad greatly impacted my ability to love my wife as she needed to be loved.

It took many years, but eventually, we came upon another great principle of marriage:

**I taught her how to love me,
and she taught me how to love her.**

How a man wants to be loved is different than how a woman wants to be loved. How a woman wants to be loved is different than how a man wants to be loved. What a fun experience we had as we practiced this principle. We discovered the purpose of marriage—being one with God and being one with each other in

We belittle God's purpose for us when we focus more on our deficiencies than on His resources.

spirit, soul, body. Shirley and I got to experience the passion of true love and not just a marriage. God taught us that loving Him would qualify us to love each other. Everything must begin with God, not with us.

We belittle God's purpose for us when we focus more on our deficiencies than on His resources.

Every purpose of God for us is based on His love for us. The greatest joy of my life was when my wife knew I loved her. The greatest fulfillment was knowing she loved me. I'm so thankful to God we never lost the passion of that love. That intense passion of our love was going to guide us through some stressful moments.

At times, great challenges come out of nowhere and your world gets turned upside down. Because the church was growing rapidly, we began a new building program in 1982. Tony was always able to see the big picture, become very excited about it, and pour himself into it. For me, the details were extremely important. He always believed God would supply no matter in what direction we would be led. As I said earlier, he believed, "Where God guides, He provides." The 18-month building program caused huge stress in our relationship, our family, and even in the church. However, we involved our children in the ministry with us every step of the journey. Sometimes all four of us would be there at night painting a room or cleaning up the construction site. Tony would hear from God and just run with the vision, and he learned a very difficult lesson:

Not everyone is reading his memos from God.

Toward the end of the project, we were all getting exhausted, and the stress was increasing to get it finished. God has given Tony an amazing gift relative to finances, in terms of raising money and dealing with bank executives. Somehow, we survived that very difficult time because of the Law of Oneness.

Not long after entering the new facility, we had another one of those stressful moments. Some of the members became disillusioned and decided to leave the ministry. One of our key staff people was included in that. To say this was a painful circumstance is to put it mildly. Tony and I took these things too personally.

However, the excitement over our new facility and the dedication of it brought a sense of unity and purpose to the church. I loved these kinds of moments! And, as you can see in the picture, I made sure that the four of us had matching outfits to look our best that day.

From that moment forward, the church grew. Several hundred people came to be partners in ministry with us. It was one of the most exciting times we had experienced since being in Toledo. Darin was involved in the music department as a drummer, and Melony was a part of the children's ministry. For us, it was a total team ministry effort. But a year later, Darin would be leaving to enter Lee University, and it was just the three of us. We handled that quite well since Melony was still with us. We always remained close with Darin despite being hundreds of miles from him. He was able to become part of the Lee Singers—a world-famous group that sang for an inauguration and also performed in London. He was truly loving this life. He left in 1985 and just two years later, Melony, who graduated a year early, headed off to Lee University. Her leaving hit us very hard because she was not only very active in the ministry, but she and I had a particularly close relationship as mother and daughter. For the first few months after she left, Tony and I had quite an adjustment to make.

In two short years, we went from four to two. I don't think we experienced the empty nest syndrome, but our lives certainly changed. Tony and I always enjoyed a very close and passionate relationship. After a few months, we began to like the fact we could spend more time and do more things together, enhancing the oneness of our relationship. As a member of the Lee Singers, Darin traveled with them while attending Lee. He graduated in 1990, and Melony graduated the following year. Melony continued to come home during the summer months and worked at the church. She had dated a young man while she was there, but she did not feel he was the person she wanted to spend her life with.

After she arrived back home, we went through one of our most challenging times at the church. Tony had spent many years mentoring the men for leadership positions by teaching them eight weeks at a time, three times a year. For whatever reason, seven of those men caused a serious conflict within the ministry, and we ended up losing more than 100 people in the congregation. Another church in the city hired away our music ministry leader, and he took half the team with him. We went from having some of the best music in town to a barely adequate music program. The betrayal by some of those men took its toll on Tony—spiritually, mentally, and physically. He lost quite a bit of weight and struggled with this betrayal for many months.

For 18 months, I prayed and sought God for an answer as to why this challenge had occurred. For years, I had poured my life into these men, and eventually, seven of them betrayed me. The toll it took on our family was devastating. To use an old cliche, I looked like death warmed over. There was little joy in my life. The loss of so many people and much musical talent greatly diminished what we were able to do in our ministry. During this time, I would lay on the floor in my office crying out to God for His help. Finally, in desperation, I screamed at God, "Why won't you heal me?" I felt like I was dying, if not physically, then surely spiritually. One day as I prayed and cried and questioned Him again about healing me of my grief, a still small voice spoke to my heart.

He said, "I cannot heal you."

I was stunned in disbelief at what I heard.

So I asked, "Why can't You heal me?"

His answer startled me. He said, "Because you have chosen to grieve, I cannot violate the choice of your will. When you choose to stop grieving, I will heal you."

At that moment, I arose from the floor and went to the restroom to wash my face with cold water. Sitting at my desk, I told God I would never grieve this incident again. It was now 18 months later, my spirit finally felt free, and I was motivated to take back everything the enemy had stolen.

Soon after this time, God sent Mario Murillo to minister in our church. Though we didn't know him personally, Tony was given his name by a friend. He had read several articles about his ministry and was impressed by how God was using Mario in His Kingdom. During that incredible seven-week period, we ended up at the Seagate Center on Halloween night with more than 4,000 people in attendance. I watched Tony walk through the most difficult period of his life, but his faith in God never wavered. He leaned hard on God, and he was strengthened by the power of God's Word to him. When it was all over, the church began to grow and multiply with new people coming almost every week.

Ministry is not for the faint of heart. Our music began to flow under new leadership, and we gained back two for one of those we lost. This was just a foretaste of what was to come in the '90s. The year 1996 was especially challenging to us on both a personal and ministry level. Earlier, I said the '90s were turbulent, and that year was the most turbulent of all. The attack this time was one of betrayal by members of our staff whom we had learned to love and trust. For sure we were going to need a deeper intimacy and a greater oneness with God than ever before. Through it all, we never gave up on the principle of **One + One = One**. Out of a great decrease came a much greater increase. For us, that was a startling revelation.

Our legacy of staying at our first church out of Lee University and raising our family here has been the deepest joy of my life. For 46 years, God has given us the honor to pastor what I believe is one of the greatest churches in the world. When people have to move away, they always say they can't find a place of worship like our home church—one that is genuine and real. Pure worship, loving Jesus, all in. I will have to say God gifted Tony with an anointing to teach the Scriptures which causes people to learn the Word and become disciplined. He always says altar calls are for people to covenant with the Word they just heard.

During these years, people have come and gone, and you must understand you can't take it personally when people leave. They make choices based on many things. We always tried to make every going out as good as it was when they were coming in. Never get so fixated on who is leaving your life that you fail to see those God is adding to you. Leave like you came is a great principle to live by. That principle works in marriage as well, and if couples lived by it, there would be fewer divorces.

We will be forever linked to God's calling on our lives. A church where people can come to experience the awesome power and Presence of God in such a way their lives are transformed is a great place to be. Our desire is that the ministry God gave us will continue to live on for generations to come. Already, the third generation is stepping forth through our granddaughters, Olivia and Mackenzie Bradley.

During this time, Shirley, Melony, and I decided to attend the Great Revival in Pensacola at Pastor John Kilpatrick's church. We flew down after having called to get an appointment to meet with him. Once we arrived, it was almost impossible to get in because of the huge crowd that had gathered early in the afternoon. His secretary told me to find her once we had entered the building, so she could introduce us to the pastor. We found a backdoor that was open and proceeded to walk in, bypassing all the crowds outside. We were seated in the front row seats because we were among the first to arrive inside the building. The service was very powerful, and the worship was heavenly. At about 90 minutes in, they took a break because the service would go almost three hours that night. During that break, I followed John Kilpatrick toward his back office, hoping to talk with him privately. I was stopped just outside his office, but I told the usher I was looking for the pastor's secretary. She just happened to be standing there. She remembered our phone conversation and tried to arrange a meeting with the pastor. Sure enough, John agreed to see us, so we went into his office.

"Pastor, how can I help you?" John asked.

"We need a move of God in Toledo, Ohio."

"Do you know what a move of God will cost you?" he asked.

"No sir, I don't, but whatever it costs I'm willing to pay the price."

We spoke for a few minutes, and he took us back into the auditorium to have the evangelist Steve Hill pray with us. All three of us were overcome by the power of the Holy Spirit. It was an extremely powerful move of God.

After the service, we went back to the hotel because we had to get up early to catch our flight to Toledo. On the flight home, we realized something dramatic was taking place in the spiritual realm. We were transformed.

So repent [change your inner self—your old way of thinking, regret past sins] and return [to God—seek His purpose for your life], so that your sins may be wiped away [blotted out, completely erased], so that times of refreshing may come from the Presence of the Lord [restoring you like a cool wind on a hot day] (Acts 3:19).

All of us need those times of refreshing in our lives. That Sunday morning at our home church was unlike anything we had ever experienced. I prayed for more than 400 people to receive a greater anointing of God's power. God impressed upon Shirley we should not go home but stay at the church and pray until the evening service. More than 100 people stayed with us to pray, and it was a breakthrough moment for so many.

God took away all my pains and hurt that day. I was healed from the wounds of those past couple of years. I truly don't remember being "called" as a pastor's wife as my husband declared he was "called" to be a pastor! I just remember being married and wanting to do whatever was needed with him as a team in ministry. When we are obedient in that way, God honors it and blesses it. God has helped me do many things I never thought I would be capable of doing. Often, I was doing things out of my gifting, and sometimes I was trying to be all things to all people. That takes a toll on you after a while, spiritually, mentally, and physically. In the beginning, I was afraid of coming up short, of not being good enough, and not meeting the demands made upon me. My experience on that Sunday of being at church all day, and the great spiritual blessing that came in Pensacola, brought great freedom in my life. From that day on, I became free, loving my life as a wife and mom, and loving God with all my heart.

Take it from someone who has been there—break free. Live your life in Christ—be who He made you to be. Serve Him through your gifts, talents, and abilities. God taught us to rest, relax, recreate, and renew. That's how He sustains us over the long haul. I learned to make myself available to God for Him to use me any way He saw fit. Prior to that time, I have to admit, I was proud of my works for His Kingdom. After that experience, I began to lead a healthy, balanced life where serving God in His Kingdom is a joy and a source of deep, personal fulfillment. Had I continued down the road I was on, ministry would have become a great burden, and there would be no peace in my heart. No question about it, Jesus taught me to stand tall in the power of His Word and the Holy Spirit. Wherever God has called you, whatever He has called you to do, you must release it into His hands. At that moment, you will experience accelerated destiny. Understanding that "oneness" is one of the laws of God's Kingdom helped us to pass it on to our children and grandchildren. Tony and I wanted nothing less than for them to know how truly being one with God enhances the marriage relationship. **One + One = One.**

Oneisms from Chapter 5

- Before you can ever experience true oneness in your marriage relationship, you must become one with Him and His purpose for you.

- A "oneness marriage" is created by a husband and wife who continuously develop intimacy, love, trust, and understanding of one another.

- Significance in life and in His Kingdom come as we are one with His purposes.

- At any given time, your challenges are permitted by God to reveal your purpose.

- Until that purpose is discovered and lived, you can never be fulfilled.

- God is always seeking to unshackle us, break the chains off us, free us, and to bring us into a relationship of oneness that fulfills us.

- When someone is loved unconditionally (mirroring Jesus), that love brings a powerful, motivating, energizing force that anchors one's soul.

- Always remember that God's love for us is unconditional, and it is also perfect. He cannot love you more than He loves you—He cannot love you less.

- Love does not produce anxiety, it cures it. Love does not injure, it heals. Love does not diminish, it increases.

Chapter 6

Oneness Increased

GOD is always ready to increase and enlarge our lives as we grasp and live the Law of Oneness. We were about to learn this in a powerful way.

In September 1998, Bishop James was having a Latter Rain Conference at the Seagate Center. He asked me and Shirley to come down on Saturday night to be a part of it. Dr. Kenneth Copeland was to be the featured speaker, and I always wanted to hear him in person. On that Thursday, Friday, and Saturday morning, Shirley and I were ministering at a mission's conference in Alabama. We arrived home late on Saturday afternoon, and I wanted to take a nap before going to the conference that evening. At about 6 p.m., I told Shirley I didn't want to go because of how tired I was, keeping in mind that we had three services the next day.

She replied, "You have to go, you promised."

Thankfully, I listened to her. We went right at 7 p.m. and slipped in the back, so we could leave early. As soon as we walked through the door, Bishop's wife was there, and she insisted we sit on the stage, front and center. (So much for being able to leave early.) God was about to divinely increase our vision with a powerful Word we have never forgotten. As I greeted Bishop James, he asked me to welcome the conference and pray. While I was speaking and then praying, Dr. Copeland came on stage and sat down in front of Shirley. Mind you, we had never met him, and he had never seen us. After he got up to speak, he tried to read his prepared text three different times—starting and stopping, pacing back and forth. Finally, he walked over to where we were sitting and began to speak these Words from God:

You plant over here in this spot and it just comes right up. You planted over there in that spot and it just came right up. My Lord God, look at these results. But there is one spot you kept planting over there and you said, "Lord, that must not have been You." The Lord said, "Yes, it was." "Well, why doesn't it come up? God, all this worked out good, all that worked out good, the ministry is so blessed, I know the ministry is blessed. Lord, if I'm standing in the way of it some way or another...." "You didn't know what was arrayed against you. You didn't miss it. You haven't failed and are not going to fail. I'm not going to let you fail," says the Lord. "No, you didn't know or understand what was arrayed against you. Heaven has it written down that you've done a good job in that area. You be faithful and you be consistent because the harvest is coming. More than your wildest dreams could ever have calculated. Because of not only your integrity but your persistence to do what God told you to do. So just rejoice and have a good time, because it's on the way!"

When Kenneth Copeland spoke the Words, "more than your wildest dreams" over Tony and me, there was no way we could have comprehended the vastness of what God was saying! From the very first day in 1974, when we drove into Toledo with our two babies, pulling our only belongings with us in a U-Haul trailer, we had a dream. It was a God-given dream that He could and would use a couple from a small town in South Carolina to persevere through the years with integrity and persistence to do what God told us to do.

We would faithfully pursue the dream no matter the forces arrayed against us. Battling the fear of failure, we always kept our eyes on the God-given dream that "Holy Toledo" would not be just a slogan, but a place out of which God would use ordinary people to do extraordinary things to touch our city and our world.

Sometimes we had to ask, "Why, God, has it taken all these years for You to process us and get us ready?" We looked at others during this time and said, "God, they have already experienced their breakthrough, their dream, and in a much shorter period of time." God would then show us that the greater the work He wants to do in us and through us, the more preparation time it takes. Many times we would say, "God, we will settle for what we are capable of handling now," not truly meaning we would give up everything God wanted to do with us and through our church.

God's vision is always bigger for us than our vision. You must remember not every good word is a God Word, but every God Word is a good Word.

"And the Lord brought Abram outside [his tent into the night] and said, 'Look now toward the heavens and count the stars—if you are able to count them.' Then He said to him, 'So [numerous] shall your descendants be'" (Genesis 15:5). Little did Abraham know that it would take 25 years for him to realize that promise.

That powerful Word from God served to motivate my efforts in His Kingdom, even to this day. That was a spiritual high like none I ever received. God answered our prayers as He continued to amaze us with increase.

One does not often equate trauma with increase. One day, I received a phone call from Darin, telling me that during a medical procedure, he had suffered a slight stroke on his left side. After finding out where he was, I called a close friend who owned a small plane to see if he could pick Darin up and bring him home to Toledo.

Thankfully, he just happened to be in the Pennsylvania area at the time, so he was very willing to help us. I met Darin at the small airport, a mile from the church, walked up into the plane, and helped him into the car. My heart was breaking. How could a healthy 30-year-old man have a stroke? We checked him into a local clinic with a renowned neurosurgeon who did a thorough examination. He found the place where there was an infarction in Darin's brain. He assured us Darin more than likely would fully recover. Over the next several weeks, I took him to rehab every day as we prayed earnestly for his healing. This took place just weeks before Christmas, and he had several musical gigs scheduled for January. God indeed had worked a miracle, and he was able to go back to his music performances, though he was still somewhat weak.

During the Christmas break, we were in South Carolina visiting relatives. I was cleaning up leaves at the condo we were staying in as I cried out to God, asking Him for a miracle. Until that moment, I would have to help Darin go to the bathroom since he could not walk on his own. I went to check on him, only to see him walking down the hallway toward the restroom by himself. God had heard our prayers. Shirley and I would realize again just how special oneness truly is.

The Words of that prophecy keep ringing in our ears: ***"You be faithful and you be consistent, because the harvest is coming . . . You didn't miss it . . . . You haven't failed and are not going to fail . . . I'm not going to let you fail . . . "*** Both of us realized how special that prophecy Dr. Copeland had given us was, and how close we must live with God to see its fruition.

With Darin on the mend, things were finally getting back to normal. From 1999-2006, we would welcome a son-in-law, a daughter-in-law, and four granddaughters. While these were very exciting and precious times for our family, there was also quite a bit of trauma. When Melony came home from a trip with Darin (she ran the product table for his traveling music group), she told us about meeting someone and believed he was the mate for her. No question about it, we were shocked. As she shared the details about what had taken place, Shirley and I were deeply concerned about her marrying someone who lived on the other side of the world (New Zealand, literally 24 hours away). We had prayed much about our children's mates. Like any good parent, we wanted to pick them. (Old Testament style!)

While Darin was at Lee, he met a young girl he believed he would marry. They had dated for several months, and he asked our family to come meet her. The young lady and her mother, along with the four of us, met for lunch. We had a nice time together, talking for quite a while.

As soon as Shirley, Melony, and I exited the restaurant's doors, I blurted out, "No way!"

"What do you mean, 'No way'?" Shirley asked. "He says he loves her."

"There is no way this can happen. There was something about the mother and the young lady that just did not feel right in my spirit," I explained.

As always, we came home and made it a matter of prayer and fasting and believed that God would somehow intervene. I tried talking to Darin about it, but he didn't want to hear it, so I prayed even harder. I felt uneasy about this relationship, and I needed God to open Darin's eyes.

Unbeknownst to me, Darin's buddy called him one night and told him to drive to a sports pub nearby. With little explanation, Darin drove there using the directions his friend had given him. This friend told Darin to go quickly, and when he arrived, to go to the back corner booth. Sure enough, as Darin walked to that booth, he saw his girlfriend making out with a young man. He left immediately, realizing the relationship was history. From that time forward, he was very wounded from the break-up. It took him several years to get over it, and he finally began to date other young ladies. Shirley and I were thrilled God intervened. While we know it wasn't possible for us to have picked their mates, it was our responsibility to know whether or not the mates they chose were right for them.

In a spirit of oneness, Shirley, Melony, and I prayed and fasted until this miracle was achieved. We did not want anyone to take away the spirit of oneness we had as a family. As we looked back to that night in Pensacola at the revival, we realized how tightly knit the three of us were. Truly, we were one in spirit. Shirley, Melony, and I loved Darin so much that we wanted more for him than this relationship would bring. Eventually, he came to see that as well.

Oneness must be increased continually to realize the full benefits of it. Perhaps, God gave us a oneness muscle that must be regularly exercised to increase its effectiveness. You don't become one at the altar when you say "I do;" you simply begin the process. That process should last a lifetime. There is nothing greater in a marriage, a home, a family than all being together—in the same book, on the same page, in the same chapter, in the same sentence, on the same word. To this day, we strive for that even during times of conflict and struggle. We want oneness to permeate every aspect of our lives beginning with our relationship with God. When we gather as a family, our focus is always on the Kingdom of God and how God wants to use us in His Kingdom. Through every storm, every trial, every challenge, the enemy's weapon is separation, division, where he tries to isolate us from one another. God's antidote for that is a spirit of oneness.

Since our family is very close, whoever our children married would need to understand the love we had for one another. To say we are close would be an understatement. During the coming months, Dave would come to Toledo to meet us and talk about his desire to marry Melony. One of my rules for performing marriage ceremonies was you had to be dating and know each other at least one year prior to the actual ceremony. Shirley and I always knew we must model the message of oneness that permeated our lives. After convincing Dave and Melony it would be at least a year, our family would then prepare for this new addition. Shirley wanted this to be a wedding for a princess because that's what Melony was to us. On September 11, 1999 (who knew what 9/11 would become), Dave and Melony were married at the church on Alexis Road to continue their journey of becoming one in spirit, soul, body. They were off to Europe on their honeymoon for two weeks as Shirley and I began adjusting to "just the two of us."

On the Sunday they departed for New Zealand after their honeymoon, we said goodbye at the gate and watched as they walked onto the plane. This was probably the most traumatic moment of our married life. Our daughter was moving to the other side of the world. We then headed back to the church to prepare for our 6 p.m. service crying all the way. What was life going to be like without the most precious daughter parents could have? She was a vital part of the ministry, and she and her mom had a very special bond—at times it was like they were sisters. They simply did everything together.

When my daughter, Melony, married and moved to New Zealand, I was having a big pity party. Here she was on the other side of the world, my son living in Tennessee, with me and Tony all alone in a city far away from our roots. This just didn't seem like a blessing to me. Normally, I had been very good at keeping negative thoughts out of my mind, but on this given Saturday (Melony and I always spent Saturdays together) I began to wallow in self-pity and cried. I feel like I have always been a strong woman, and I can normally handle whatever comes my way. On Saturday nights, Melony and I would have a phone conversation (Sunday for her in New Zealand). I was not upbeat and strong during that conversation, and it began to come out as I told her about my rough day, missing her.

She said, "Mom, I'm sorry you're having a rough day. I will pray even harder for you. Someday we'll all understand why it has to be this way for a season."

Needless to say, when I hung up, I was angry with myself for not being strong enough, for not keeping my mouth closed, and perhaps even discouraging Melony. Sometime later when the family was together, Tony shared something that God had spoken to him. He, like myself, struggled greatly with our kids being away from us, especially Melony being on the other side of the world. In his office, on his face before God, he was complaining about this very thing, when suddenly, God spoke to him.

He said, "That which you accept in your life, you will no longer be challenged to change."

Tony looked each of us in the eye and said, "No matter how far from each other or how busy we may be, we must not accept the fact of not being together often. We must make a covenant with one another to come together at least five times a year. Your mom and I will come to you twice, you will come to us twice, and we will meet somewhere together at least once."

This we practiced for many years to come.

Years ago, my mom and I attended a women's conference in California.

As we sat with a group at dinner, my friend Jackie said, "Shirley, I want you to know how much I appreciate the way you always take care of your mom. You bring her with you to conferences like this and other international meetings. You are such a wonderful example of how a daughter should treat her mother and take care of her."

Looking back now, I was being an example to my own daughter, and she has done the same for me, as her daughters watch how she treats me.

It was now the year 2000, and Darin informed us of meeting a young woman, an Australian, whom he planned to marry. Once again, our family was increasing, yet we want to retain the oneness and the closeness that we have had through the years. Darin and Bronwyn were married on the Big Island in Hawaii in February 2001. All of us traveled there since it was the halfway point to Australia. The Hitzke family and the Scott family came together for a beautiful oceanside wedding. Soon we would all go our separate ways—Dave and Melony to New Zealand, Darin and Bronwyn to Nashville, and Shirley and I back to Toledo. The emptiness syndrome honestly did not affect us because we understood oneness. I was enough for her, and she was enough for me, even though we missed our children.

In the summer of 2001, we were finishing up our Sunday morning service when someone notified me Melony had sent a video for us to see. Our video team started the video, and Dave and Melony gave the surprise announcement that we were going to be grandparents. Amazing joy and excitement filled our hearts that day. And on January 16th, 2002, Olivia Ann Bradley was born. Again, we faced some trauma as she was six weeks premature. Two months earlier, Melony and Dave had been on a camping retreat in Australia for a business function. One day, Melony slipped and fell, landing very hard. She seemed to be okay and came to the states a few weeks later to prepare for the birth of her first child. Shortly after arriving home, Melony experienced complications that landed us in the hospital.

After a thorough examination, the doctor came in and said, "It appears her fall caused a blood clot to form, and Melony and the baby are in danger if we don't take action now."

I told the doctor we must pray first. The tears began to flow as I asked God for His help protecting Melony and the baby, and guiding the surgeon.

When I finished praying, the doctor too was teary-eyed and said, "I pray that I will love my daughter as I can see you love yours."

Melony and Olivia had to remain in the hospital for several days after her successful birth. She has been healthy ever since. One could view this as an attack from the enemy or maybe God allowed us to see the complication so the blood clot could be removed and thus preserve their lives.

Our trauma was magnified when I found out the wear and tear on my vocal cords through the years had produced a nodule that must be surgically removed. So, during a time of great joy and celebration, we were faced with going to Vanderbilt University, where one of the major vocal cord surgeons in the world practiced. Singers from around the world would come there to have Dr. Ossoff perform vocal cord surgeries. The miracle of this story is that a friend of mine told me of him, so I called to get an appointment. His assistant shared with me he was booked up, and it was near impossible to take on any new patients. I persisted in my conversation and told her I lived in Toledo, and I would be coming there for the surgery.

"Oh, I used to live in Ohio. And since you're a Buckeye, I'm going to work you in." Throughout our lives, we have seen these God moments which only He can set up.

Truly, it was a great miracle. We traveled to Nashville three weeks after Olivia's birth for my surgery. During the consultation, Dr. Ossoff informed me there were no guarantees on how well the surgery would work.

"You will never get your full voice back completely, but I will do the best I can. It may only be 65 to 70 percent."

I would have to do exactly what he told me after the operation. There would be no speaking for two weeks after the surgery. And then, I would speak only a few words a day for the next couple of weeks. Once the surgery was complete, we traveled back to Toledo, so I could begin four weeks of rehab. He required me to return to Nashville every two weeks and to abstain from teaching for at least three months. The long process took its toll on me and after six weeks, I felt strong enough to at least share a few minutes and not strain my voice. Over the next few months, my voice continued to improve, but not to the point I desired. Before the surgery, one of my intercessors shared with me a Word God gave her, which simply said: "You will recover all." After about nine months of doing therapy and rehab on a daily basis, I was speaking on a Sunday morning and in the middle of the message, my voice changed—God had performed a miracle. I recovered it. I recovered all.

While I cannot speak for others, had Shirley and I not experienced the principle of **One** + **One** = **One**, the traumas we went through could have had a very negative effect upon our marriage and family. As we look back on each of these events, it seemed God deepened our understanding of oneness with each other. Oftentimes, trauma, conflict, and challenges will divide a husband and wife. We were intentional by not letting this happen to us. Yes, we had conflicts and yes, the pressures of life got to us at times, but I can tell you we never considered for a moment not being together. (We never considered divorce, but she might have thought of murder a few times! You know, until death do us part.) We were committed to the oneness principle. Nothing would ever come between us (or between us and our children) for which we couldn't find a solution. Our focus was God, our family, and His church. That's what oneness will do for you. In becoming one, you limit the effects of the enemy's attacks. That is why God gave us the oneness principle in the very first marriage. Positive or negative, good or bad, God wants this oneness to be greatly increased on our life's journey.

As Dave, Melony, Darin, and Bronwyn grew their marriage relationships, our desire was for them to become one as Shirley and I were one. In 2003, Darin and Bronwyn welcomed Bella into our family. Thankfully, we were there at the hospital when she was born. One year later, Dave and Melony welcomed Mackenzie, our third grand-daughter. In 2006, Abbie was born, and we were informed our family was now complete. I protested we could not stop with four girls, and that we needed a boy. My protest went unanswered. Yet, there is no way I could love a grandson more than I love these four granddaugh-ters. Each of them is unique and special in their own right.

Our family is complete!
Here we are enjoying lunch after Easter services—all ten of us!

In 2006, Dave and Melony moved from their home in New Zealand to live near us in Toledo. Melony resumed her position as administrator at the church as Dave continued to build his network marketing business. No one was more thrilled than Shirley. It had been her dream we would all work together in the ministry. Over the next couple of years, we moved into side-by-side condos just three minutes from the church. We were two families living almost as one and eating dinner every night together. She was loving every minute of it. God had given Shirley her heart's desire and honored her faithfulness to Him. Shirley, Melony, and the girls enjoyed their Saturday excursions to shop, have coffee, or just be together.

The most important relationships are those found in the home. The best part of life is who we get to do life with. Our family members determine the thermometer of our lives and our ministry. Life is not about stuff as much as it is about people, relationships, and wisdom.

Mother Teresa was once given an award for her achievements by the President of the United States. She was asked this question, "What do you think is the single greatest thing we can do to bring world peace?" She answered, "Simple, love your family, build relationships with your wife and your children, then just watch the thing explode."

Grandparenthood has been one of life's greatest joys for Tony and me. It is the greatest surprise awaiting every parent in the empty nest stage of life. I never knew I could love so deeply until I first laid eyes on my granddaughter Olivia Ann in the delivery room. I once heard someone say, "I can't say you are good until I see your grandkids."

At the time of this writing, Tony and I are at the age where it would be easy to sit back and relax and enjoy the beauty and comfort of retirement. But no, here we are still fully all in. Life in His Kingdom on Earth and in the church have never been more exciting. We listen and pursue God. When will it end? Only God knows. We have thought about stopping several times but there is no retirement, for the prophets never retire. I know one thing—the saint of God never dies—we are either alive with Christ on this Earth or alive with Him in Heaven.

We have enjoyed a rich and full life, filled with God's richest blessings. From the beginning of our life together, we dedicated and consecrated ourselves and our family 100 percent to the call of God. We laid our lives on His altar and have never picked them back up again.

Tony and I decided nothing would ever steal the promise that our family's destiny is ordained by God. God brought us all back together, and for 14 years I've had the privilege of seeing two of my beautiful granddaughters every day of my life. During this time, the six of us developed a beautiful oneness of spirit, soul, body that permeates our lives daily. Because of oneness, a covenant bond was created.

Our oldest granddaughter, Olivia, whom we call the Queen (she was the firstborn), began to show a remarkable talent for music. She wanted to play the violin, clarinet, guitar, and piano. She also discovered she really likes to sing and has a beautiful voice. As we were developing this spiritual oneness, both of Melony's daughters began to discover the Kingdom gifts God had placed within them. We created an atmosphere of loving and serving God. And out of that atmosphere, a love was born in their hearts to do His Kingdom work alongside us. Mackenzie loves working with children, even at a young age, and the children truly love her. To say these times were like a dream is to put it mildly. I always wanted my family to be involved in the ministry with me and Tony. God has granted that request.

From the time Olivia was born to when she was 13 years of age, a spirit of fear threatened to ruin her life. She never spent a night away from home (no sleepovers), and she would get very afraid when a storm would pass through. Many nights she would end up sleeping with her mom. At times, she would break into tears and be inconsolable. Through the years, Tony and I prayed earnestly for God to deliver her. And in 2015, a great miracle took place. It was the week-long summer camp for our youth, and Tony would always speak to them and pray over them on the second night of camp.

When he stepped in front of Olivia, the Lord spoke through him and said, "Tonight, I am delivering you from your spirit of fear. And to the degree to which you have been fearful, you will now be bold."

The two of them were crying as God manifested His Presence mightily in her life. And bold she became. A few weeks after, school started and Olivia was sharing her miracle with a few classmates. The teacher overheard her and asked if she would share with all of the students. It wasn't long after that the principal was made aware, and she was asked to share her great deliverance for the school's chapel. The difference that evening made in her life was like night and day. God gave her a thirst for His Kingdom that has never been quenched. She rose up to become one of the key spiritual leaders at Toledo Christian School, greatly admired by staff, teachers, and students alike. Young people were drawn to her, and she would pray for them.

Today, Olivia is enrolled in The Ramp School of Ministry in Hamilton, Alabama, where God is using her for His glory! Already she has composed a song that wonderfully glorifies God, and she is a leader among the students.

Mackenzie, her sister, also found her place in the Kingdom as she began to teach the younger children. She has now assumed the role of Assistant Children's Director at our church while just a teenager. The oneness of God's Spirit was increasing in our family, and it was a beautiful thing to observe. Oneness should flow from one genera-tion to the next.

This miracle can be experienced by you, by anyone who will determine in their hearts.

When people ask us how this all came to be—that our children and grandchildren love God so much—we tell them it was intentional. Our goal, our dream, was that we would be a ministry family of Kingdom servants living in a covenant with God and with each other.

This miracle can be experienced by you, by anyone who will determine in their hearts.

"As for me and my house, we will serve the Lord"
(Joshua 24:15 NIV).

It is never too late to start and see what God can do in your life and with the ones you love. You will discover oneness is a process by which God runs His Kingdom and wants you to run your life. You too can learn about covenant—a covenant marriage, a covenant family, a covenant ministry. He is a covenant God and has chosen to make covenants with us. It may well be the greatest principle we have ever learned and lived.

First comes the Law of Oneness, **One + One = One**, and then the all-consuming Law of Covenant.

Oneisms from Chapter 6

- ♥ God often produces increase out of trauma.

- ♥ There is nothing greater in a marriage, a home, a family than a spirit of unity—in the same book, on the same page, in the same chapter, in the same sentence, on the same word.

- ♥ Through every storm, every trial, every challenge, the enemy's weapon is separation, division, where he tries to isolate us from one another. God's antidote for that is a spirit of oneness.

- ♥ That which you accept in your life, you will no longer be challenged to change.

- ♥ In becoming one, you limit the effects of the enemy's attacks. That is why God gave us this oneness principle in the beginning. Positive or negative, good or bad, God wants this principle to continually increase on our life's journey.

Part 3:

The Secret of Covenant Living

Chapter 7

Covenant Is Everything

FROM the beginning of time, God introduced a way of life called covenant. As you go through the pages of the Bible, you will see God entering into a covenant with man concerning His will on Earth. Covenant entails everything you are involved in—marriage, family, occupation, business, friendships, and relationships. How we live our lives and how we respond to others on Earth should be governed by covenant Kingdom principles that enrich and enhance us as well as others. When you live covenant, you can expect God to back up your living. It will enable you to conquer life's challenges.

Poet William Ernest Henley suffered the loss of a foot and ankle due to disease. In his pain and suffering, he wrote the poem "Invictus," meaning "unconquered."

> **"I am the master of my fate;**
> **I am the captain of my soul."**

Obviously, that is not how God intended for our story to be written or yours. He wants to be the Master of our fates and the Captain of our souls.

No one will ever understand God who doesn't grasp the concept of covenant. He is forever a covenant God and only deals with man on the basis of covenant. To be in covenant means to value someone else's life as much as you value yours. Shirley and I were beginning to understand our story was interwoven with His-story for us. We knew God is never an editor. He writes, produces, and directs His-story for our lives. Our ordinary stories become extraordinary when we live in covenant with Him. We were often surprised by how nothing in our human story was *ever* wasted. He uses whatever happens to us to expand His Kingdom through living grace. Any time you don't like your story, you can change the script and create a new role, with a new plot (a new plan). While it is true you can never change your beginning, you can start now and write a new ending. William Cowper wrote a great hymn entitled "God Moves in a Mysterious Way."

**"God moves in a mysterious way, His wonders
to perform; He plants His footsteps in the sea
and rides upon the storm. Deep in unfathomable
mines of never-failing skill, He treasures up
His bright designs and works His sovereign will . . . .
His purposes will ripen fast, unfolding every hour;
the bud may have a bitter taste,
but sweet will be the flower."**

He disciplines us, educates us, and trains us as we interact with the forces of everyday life. His education always involves the development of our mental capabilities, gifts, and powers in perfect harmony with His will.

His purpose involves the following:

the strengthening and disciplining of our intellect,
the stimulating and directing of our emotions,
the undergirding of our conscience,
the training of our will,
and the discipline of our body.

As we practice these spiritual disciplines, we are brought into servanthood for the worthy purpose of His Kingdom. God is a master at taking insignificant human stories and making them significant divine stories.

As children growing up in textile mill villages in South Carolina, nothing about our lives revealed any information concerning what God had in store for us. Church was always a big part of our lives. Serving God was a settled issue that was never up for discussion. But always inside of us, there was a deeper interest in God and His ways and purpose for us. "The big picture" always attracted our attention to our God-ordained destiny. Mind you, we had no true understanding of what a true covenant with God meant at this time. We would learn that covenant truly is everything in serving God in His Kingdom. Covenant is a wide-open door into an intimate and personal relationship with God, in which He reveals the deep things of His Spirit.

Psalm 25:14 says, "Fear Him, and He will let them know His covenant *and* reveal to them [through His Word] its [deep, inner] meaning."

Imagine God choosing two young people from a small southern town and anointing us for Kingdom ministry. He sent us to Toledo, Ohio, to preach and teach His Gospel of the Kingdom for the past 46 years, even as far away as Korea, Japan, the Philippines, Africa,

> God has given us a guiding principle: Our reach must always exceed our grasp—this is only possible when you understand and live covenant.

Germany, New Zealand, Australia, and Canada. He can do the same and even more for anyone who is willing to persevere and follow their Kingdom purpose.

When we arrived in Toledo in 1974 along with our son, Darin, and daughter, Melony, the church was small (50 adults) and its vision obscured. Today, 46 years later, we are on a beautiful 57-acre campus, theChurch is international in scope with a weekly television ministry, online streaming, and another campus in Fremont, Ohio. Literally, tens of thousands of people are touched on a yearly basis.

God has given us a guiding principle: Our reach must always exceed our grasp—this is only possible when you understand and live covenant.

My father and mother were not Christians when I was born. When I was about 12 years old, they were invited to attend church on a Sunday at Tremont Avenue Church of God in Greenville, South Carolina, by my uncle, who had recently given his heart to God. My parents started taking Sharon, my sister, and me to church, and this is really where it all started for me. I am so thankful I was raised in a Christian home and taught to go to church every week. I hate to think where I would be today and what my life would look like if someone had not witnessed to my father, who became the first one in his family to receive Christ. This is a miracle in itself because my dad's family was so lost without God and really deep into sin. Without this story, I don't really know what my journey would be. As my dad began to serve in his church, he drew closer and closer to God and started to feel a calling on his life to preach. He would teach the men's Bible class on Sundays and go out on the street corners and preach and witness to people. Soon he was given a church to pastor called Paris Mountain Church of God. This was the beginning of his ministry which led to our journey. For 40 years, my mom and dad obeyed God and went on to pastor several churches in South Carolina, and this is how I was fortunately raised as a Christian. I cannot imagine our family not being saved, my dad not being a pastor, and me not being at that youth camp on that very special day when I met Tony. His mom was a godly saint and lived a covenant life with God. So strong was her covenant that she never took so much as an aspirin—totally trusting God to heal her of any sickness or disease. We were being introduced to what a covenant life looked like, so we would later come to understand that covenant living is the highest life.

Never doubt that your divine story is far greater than your human story could ever be. That transition requires divine alignment. God permits changes in our lives to remove options, and makes it easier for us to do His will completely. Perhaps I should warn you that divine alignment in our lives is never without pain. God did not ask Joseph if he wanted to be put into prison. He did not ask Daniel if he wanted to be placed into the lion's den. He didn't ask David if he wanted to be hunted like an animal by King Saul. He didn't ask Paul if he was willing to lose his life for the sake of the Kingdom. God never asks permission to bring us into divine alignment. He narrows our options to bring us to a choice of living His-story or living our own.

Not long after finishing our first building project in 1976, a young lady came to our church, along with her three children. I would later become aware that her father was the owner of a Fortune 500 company worth hundreds of millions of dollars. Prior to her coming, I had actually been in his office selling church bonds in order to finish up our new gymnasium. In an article written in *The Toledo Blade* newspaper, I saw his picture for the first time. While praying about money for the gym, I felt impressed to see if he would purchase some of our church bonds. I went to his office to meet him and something inside me said, "He will help you," and help me he did. He later would tell me that he had no interest in the bonds, but he would give us $10,000 if we let him. Two days later, the check arrived. Over the next 20 years, he would sow more than $600,000 into our ministry. The final check was for more than one quarter of a million dollars after his death. When you live in covenant with God, you experience miraculous things in every arena of life. This miracle of finance was over-the-top. Had I not been obedient to God's voice, this miracle would not have happened. That one act of obedience, listening to His still small voice, gave us the money to purchase our new facility. God was teaching me a covenant principle: obedience. Covenant is everything.

Our story was about to see several major challenges. At the time, they didn't seem so significant to us, but as we looked back, they altered the course of our lives and ministry. When I became aware that I had some physical issues, we scheduled an appointment at the medical clinic.

The doctor came in to meet with us and said, "Your blood pressure is very high, and I want you to begin blood pressure medication today."

This was in January of 1997. God had impressed upon me that the church was to enter into a 40-day period of prayer and fasting. I asked Tony to pray about this. He made the decision to begin this on January the 2nd, and we asked the church to join us. When the doctor said we must start the medicine, we told him about our time of prayer and fasting. I can't say he liked it, but he agreed for me to wait until this fast was over. He would, after this time, check my blood pressure again. Tony had heard about a man named Kim Clement and the great move of God's Spirit in Detroit. Melony came with us to attend a service. Kim did not know us, and we did not know him—we had never seen each other.

Toward the end of the service, he looked over to where we were sitting and said, "This family right here—come up front," as he pointed to the three of us.

That night he spoke to us about my family (my parents' families) having numerous heart conditions and diseases.

The Lord said directly to me, "It ends with you."

Needless to say, we were overwhelmed by God's Presence and His sure Word of prophecy. Kim had no way of knowing anything about us, let alone my recent medical diagnosis. After the prayer and fasting ended, miraculously, my blood pressure was normal. That night began an almost 20-year relationship with Kim. He spoke many things over us, including the fact that we would have a new church facility we wouldn't have to build. Later, he came to speak at our church and would return multiple times during the next several years. On one of those occasions, he spoke the following to us:

"Preparation has taken place. Visitation has come to you," says the Lord. "But your visitation has come to an end and you have passed the test. Now comes divine habitation. I will possess you and I will fill this city with My glory, because you have passed the test," says the Lord. Hallelujah! "What you've got to understand is that you cannot contain the glory in this building. It has to be outside of this building." And the Spirit of the Lord says, "There is something better that I have already raised up. It's already out there. I will use this for another feature. I will use this place for another thing and another time. But there's something out there that I personally will build," says the Lord. "And when I build it, it will be a light that will shine not only in this city and in the district that surrounds you, but to different states, even across the border into Canada. I will release you into a realm of a greater measure of rule. Your measure of rule, your faith, has been expounded and has gone to a greater

degree. *I am building something for you. I am preparing land for you. No, not just one but various pieces,"* says the Lord. *"All over, so that they will be literally a compass of My glory. North, south, east, and west where there will be houses built up. This is not a house of prophetic utterance only, but this is an apostolic order that has been raised up within this house that I will cause the people to say, 'Let us go to that place because God is doing something different. He's not doing the normal. The miracles that are happening there are not redundant. They are fresh, they are new, they are creative.' They will say, "Even people that are dying of AIDS are getting healed. They will say strange miracles are taking place. You will draw the medical profession, and you will cause medical science to come in and inspect what has happened." And God says, "I will be proven once again that I am Jehovah. I am the Healer. I will be proven once again that I am able to do exceeding abundantly above all that you ask or can imagine. I am able,"* says the Lord. *"A house is about to be built that will affect the entire nation. Rejoice, because this is who you are,"* says the Lord. The Spirit of the Lord says, *"There is a place for you. There's a holy place for you and Toledo shall be holy."*

On a Friday night in November 2003, Tony and I came home just to rest and relax after an exhausting week of ministry.

At about 6 p.m., he said, "I think I will go to Detroit to hear Kim speak tonight."

Being somewhat tired and just wanting to rest, I encouraged him to go. Tony's heart always hungers for more of God, and he saw something in Kim that made him eager to learn from him. He proceeded to freshen up and get ready to go when I had a strong feeling I should go with him. We traveled to the hotel ballroom across from the airport in Detroit. Arriving right at 7 p.m., we decided to sit in the back, so we could slip out toward the end of the service. Once his team members saw us, they insisted we sit in front where they had some seats reserved. Kim came out to play the piano and sing as others joined in a time of worship. About 30 minutes into the worship, he arose from the piano and began looking for someone. Though we had maintained contact with him, we had not physically seen him in five years.

He looked down on the front row. "Tony and Shirley—stand up, God has a Word for you!"

With tears streaming down our faces, he began to speak, "What is this I hear? Who shall be my heir? Who shall take over the ministry when I am gone?"

And the Lord says, "Your heir shall come out of your loins."

Tony later told me those were his exact words to God over the last couple of years. We were working hard to build a great ministry, and he was concerned about who would take over for him when he would no longer continue as the lead pastor.

He said, "Shirley, I was shocked when Kim spoke those exact words of my prayer." Jokingly, he said to me, "Does this mean we need to have another baby?"

To which I quickly replied, "Don't be silly."

He joked, "Come on, Sarah—have faith."

Something happened in 2005 which caused us to see what God meant.

Kim also said, "God has already raised up a building for you—one you won't need to build."

We had been intently looking for a place or land to move into. Tony tried to buy Northtown Mall in Toledo which had been closed for a few years. He made an offer for $5,000,000 which was rejected. Within six months, the mall sold for $750,000. He was very confused as to how his larger offer had been refused and the

$750,000 offer had been accepted. We know now it was God. A company purchased declining malls across the country to redevelop them. Our attention was turned to land in Michigan—a total of 40 acres. The church made an offer to buy the land, and it was accepted. Two weeks later we were informed our acceptance in writing had actually been rejected. By now it was 2005, and we were wondering about this new facility God had planned for us.

His-story for us is ever expanding and filled with new adventures. Our property on Alexis Road had served us well since 1983. We built it with our own hands, hiring laborers to help us along the way. I spoke previously of the stress it had on our family, marriage, and even the church, so getting back into the building program was not enticing to me and Shirley. Over a period of five years, three different servants of God had spoken to us about God raising a place we would not have to construct. On a Wednesday night service, a young woman named Kay Ziegler came to the altar to pray with a desire that she and her husband would be used by God for His Kingdom purposes. His name was Jeff, and he was already a successful real estate developer. In my morning prayer time, I felt God impress upon my heart to ask for Jeff's help in finding a new location for the church. I shared this with Kay, and she shared it with Jeff. On Sunday morning, he came to the altar for prayer with Kay. I shared with Jeff what God had spoken to me concerning enlisting his help. Over the next several days, we spoke about the acreage, size of the building, etc., that would be needed. While he was golfing in a tournament several weeks later, he inquired about property from a man named Marty Gallagher, a commercial real estate owner.

Marty said, "I think I know just the place you're looking for."

He and Jeff looked at the facility and invited me to come and tour the building. When I first drove up (I had never seen the place before), I was struck by the beautiful landscaping of the facility. Formerly occupied by an auto parts manufacturer, the building was situated on 57 acres with more than 120,000 square feet. At first, I felt we were wasting our time since there was no way we could afford such a facility. It took 45 minutes to walk through the building. Beautifully designed with more than 300 windows, it had that natural, earth-like feel to it. When we came to the end of the tour, I asked how much they wanted for the building. Marty had inquired, and they indicated an offer of 15 million would be needed. The company had been purchased by the Eton Corporation, and this facility was mothballed as they already had a world headquarters building. An insurance company owned it and was owed $13.2 million of the remaining lease. Since the new company had no use for the building, they were looking for a way out. Negotiations had not been fun with the insurance company, and the lessee had to come to some kind of agreement that would satisfy all parties. It took more than a year, but we ended up getting the facility for $7,000,000. Perhaps this was one of our greatest miracles—as we got to move into a $20,000,000 facility for one third the price. Through the years, I became aware that God had gifted me with financial wisdom and expertise. With that knowledge, I understood how to negotiate financing, find money, and raise money. This project was going to challenge me in ways I never encountered before. Local Toledo banks didn't feel, even at such a low price, we were financially strong enough to handle the mortgage. Of course, our track record was quite impressive, always paying off every loan within seven to eight years. At the time, we had accumulated over $750,000 in our savings toward a new facility.

You can't imagine the excitement we had concerning this development in our story. This new world-class facility had a restaurant, four conference rooms, 68 classrooms, 18 bathrooms, beautiful landscaping, and a pond. We could hardly believe our eyes. Because of Tony's abilities with finance, we were able to purchase the building for one third its value. May I just say, covenant is everything. This was beyond our wildest imaginings and a direct result of learning to live in covenant in Him. Needless to say, we were overwhelmed and humbled by God's generosity to us. Not one day has gone by, as we drive on this campus, that we are not reminded of how faithful He is to those who humble themselves in His Presence. The Word Kim spoke over us was coming to pass and beyond anything I dreamed our new building would be.

Financing the new building was one of the biggest challenges of my life to date. Toledo area banks turned me down.

The president of KeyBank looked me in the eye and said, "I know you will pull this off, but there is no way the home office will let me take on this loan with your church."

As I have learned to do throughout my life, I prayed and fasted for an answer from God. Beginning in the early '90s, I was given the privilege of serving on the board for the International Church of God and served every year I was eligible—22 years. During that time, we often heard from great leaders in various fields such as church growth, church construction, and church financing. One man's name stuck out to me, and I gave him a call to see if he knew of a bank that would loan money for such a project as this. He had a contact with a bank in Walnut Grove, California, and told me to use his name as a reference. To my knowledge, this was the only bank in the nation with a church loan division. After contacting this individual and having him look at the facility, he arranged for the president of the church loan division to come and assess the building. He was somewhat blown away by the world-class facility and said he would like to be a part of it, but he wasn't sure we qualified. However, God provided the miracle, and they gave us the loan at a very low interest rate.

During the next 18 months, we experienced overwhelming miracles that would take our breath away—almost beyond belief. Purchasing the building and remodeling it had taken its toll on our cash flow, and we were unable to borrow any more money. Our old, original facility on Alexis Road was under contract for 3.5 million dollars, and the people backed out the day before closing. Over the next few months, we would experience a deficit of over $60,000 per month. Shirley became very concerned over the financial stress and what it was doing to me physically.

Although God had provided several miracles to get us into the new building, it seemed we needed a miracle every month to remain here. Tony is adamant about paying bills on time and maintaining a great credit rating. He thrives under great challenge because he will continuously pray and fast until an answer comes from Him. And did God ever supply the miracle!

In February 2006, Dr. T.L. Lowery—our mentor, friend, and pastor—came to speak at the church. A close friend had flown him up for the weekend. This man was greatly blessed by God in building a huge business that he sold for hundreds of millions of dollars. Tony and I had never met him. Between the 9 a.m. and 11 a.m. service, Tony, Dr. Lowery, and his friend were in the office talking about the beauty and possibilities of the facility.

The friend asked Tony, "What is your greatest need?"

Tony simply replied, "Cash flow."

As the 11 a.m. service began, Tony asked Dr. Lowery to introduce his friend. While this man was sharing with the church God's blessing on his life, he asked me to come up on stage with Tony. He shared with the congregation how God had blessed him abundantly, and he liked to invest in the building of God's Kingdom. He prayed for Tony and me and handed us a check which Tony briefly looked at but couldn't make out the numbers because of his tears.

I whispered to him, "Tony, it's $500,000!"

"No way," he gasped.

It was indeed! Immediately, some side notes we had borrowed were paid in full, and we now had money to operate on for several months. You can see why Tony and I feel so strongly about covenant living. Covenant truly is everything to those who live it, especially in relationships. God introduced covenant living in the Garden of Eden and revealed to us covenant love on the pages of the Bible. Only when you grasp the full meaning of covenant will you be able to live in absolute trust of His love for you.

Jesus gave us a new covenant—a blood covenant—in His suffering, death, and resurrection. To this day, I still pray and speak the blood covenant of Jesus over people, places, and things. However, covenant living is not without challenges, as we were about to experience.

Oneisms from Chapter 7

- ♥ No one will ever understand God who doesn't grasp the concept of covenant.

- ♥ God is a master at taking insignificant human stories and making them significant divine stories.

- ♥ Covenant is a wide-open door into an intimate and personal relationship with God in which He reveals the deep things of His Spirit. Covenant causes us to come into divine alignment with His plans and purposes.

- ♥ Never doubt that your divine story is far greater than your human story could ever be.

- ♥ God narrows our options to bring us to a choice of living His-story or living our own.

- ♥ Always listen to the still small voice of God in your spirit.

Chapter 8

Covenant Is Challenging

COVENANT living is how God designed life to be lived, but it comes with many challenges. He is a covenant God and only deals with man on the basis of that. His intentions for us are to live covenant lives with our fellow sojourners on Earth.

The words of David in Psalm 73:11-14 (MSG) sum up the challenge for us:

> What's going on here? Is God out to lunch? Nobody's tending the store. The wicked get by with everything; they have it made, piling up riches. I've been stupid to play by the rules; what has it gotten me? A long run of bad luck, that's what— a slap in the face every time I walk out the door.

Without question, God had ordained our purchase of this facility. We had weathered the initial cash flow shortages and the church was really growing. People are often mesmerized by the beauty of our campus. Daily, it seems like we are driving into a beautiful resort.

There are three truths that impact my life on a daily basis:

1. Nothing gets into my life or affects me without coming through His hands.

2. Whatever He permits into my life, is meant to increase me, not diminish me.

3. Just because something is God's will doesn't guarantee success.

Somewhere I read it is unnecessary to state the obvious, but I will anyway: **Sometimes covenant living isn't fair.**

When the Bible calls the enemy our adversary, it is referring to an opponent in a lawsuit—one who will slander and accuse us. By 2008-2009, our country suffered a financial meltdown. Great banks and lending institutions went under as millions were impacted nationwide—you probably felt that too. Unemployment soared and soon we were faced with a half-million-dollar decrease annually in income. At one point, our unemployment rate was above 18 percent in Lucas County. Often the attacks of the enemy make life unjust and simply not fair.

Through it all, I tried to remain calm and steadfast in believing that God had guided us here, and He would provide. It was then He taught me an amazing truth concerning faith.

On a Saturday morning, I was in my office praying. The financial pressures were so great that only an answer from God would get us through. It didn't seem my prayers were going anywhere. A bitter complaint came rolling out of my mouth concerning my obedience to purchase property that He led us to.

Finally, I sat down in my chair and said to God, "I am not getting up until You answer me."

Then a still small voice spoke to my spirit, **"I cannot respond to the language of your doubt. I can only respond to the language of your faith."**

My response to God: "I don't know what faith is."

He impressed me to open my Bible and begin reading The Creation Story. As I was reading it...day one, day two, all the way to day six...I stopped.

He said, "Read on," and He asked me this question: "What did I do after I spoke the Universe into existence?"

"You rested," I replied.

He said to me, "You will be in faith when you speak My Word over the situation and then rest."

Perseverance always outlasts persecution.

That was one of the most profound things God ever spoke into my heart. Though my covenant was challenged, I persevered.

Perseverance always outlasts persecution.

Leo Tolstoy once said, "It is by those who have suffered that the world has advanced."

The dark places of life must become for us the birthplace of vision. Suddenly, it dawned on me that our great challenge

Never permit the shadow of life's unfairness to limit the vision of your tomorrow.

caused a sense of unfairness within me and greatly affected my attitude. A negative reaction to your circumstance can cause emotional paralysis and can even cause regression into your past.

Never permit the shadow of life's unfairness to limit the vision of your tomorrow.

A positive, active, creative response that would bring growth and development was urgently needed.

With our nation having suffered through a massive economic downturn, the casting of vision to move the church forward was challenging. I came to realize that giving might never return to the levels it had been at before. During this time, God had sent a CPA to the church named Kristal Saneda. Kristal had been involved in investments with a national company. God had greatly gifted her with an understanding of budgeting, finance, and the management of funds. She came alongside me, and together we planned out a financial future for the church. Immediately, we were faced with the challenge of eliminating a quarter of a million dollars from our yearly budget. Since we had always been very frugal and tight-fisted with our money, this was not going to be easy. Kristal's love for God and His Kingdom work served as a motivation for her involvement in the ministry.

"Money follows ministry" is a principle
I believed in strongly.

In the process of making budget cuts, we had to make sure we did not diminish ministry to the needs of the people. Covenant love had always been the driving force through our ministry goals and programs. Shirley was the heart and soul of this effort. She had the heart of Jesus for the neediest of people. He said, "I have come so that the poor will have the Gospel preached to them." The core message of the Gospel is sharing His love. No one was better than showing this truth than Shirley.

For more than 30 years, we had thrown a big birthday party in the central city at Christmas called The Noel Project. As a kid growing up, I never got a new bicycle. While the neighborhood kids rode their new bikes at Christmas, I either didn't have one or had a used one my dad purchased somewhere. Since he was an alcoholic, there was seldom any money for family Christmas gifts. Not ever having a new bike left a scar on my soul, and I wanted the church to bring love and joy to those less fortunate. The Noel Project was growing each year, and we were giving away over 500 bicycles at Christmas, along with a toy for each child, a turkey dinner, coats, and hats. At the time, the project was costing us more than $50,000. One of the elders suggested foregoing The Noel Project that particular year since our income had diminished significantly. It was something I just couldn't do. The burden of financing the project each year was mainly my responsibility. Since I was never one who was timid or shy about doing the business of the Kingdom, we forged ahead, and God came through. Miraculously, we pulled through those two or three years without ever missing a payment on our building, and we continued to increase the ministry for others. Slowly but surely, we were growing out of our financial challenge while remaining true to our Kingdom covenant.

But once again, covenant is often challenged. An interesting scenario took place with the bank that held our mortgage. Though we had an excellent credit rating, always paying our notes off well in advance of maturity, and never missing a mortgage payment, we were not meeting the formula that was written into our contract. One day I received a notification saying the president of the bank needed to meet with me. When she came that day, there were two men with her I did not know. We met in the conference room, where they sat at the end of the table. Kristal was with me at that meeting. Because we had not met the technical aspects of our mortgage, they wanted me to know the loan was no longer desirable for them. We were heavy on assets but only adequate with our cash flow. Truthfully, the two men looked like mafia people to me. I was told they would be taking over the note in the Detroit office of the bank, and we would answer to them. When the meeting was over and they left, I asked Kristal for her thoughts.

She said, "It's a noncompliant note because we are not meeting the technicalities written into the contract."

She knew we had never missed a payment, nor made a payment late, but she understood the bank's challenge. We were scheduled to meet again in a couple of weeks, and the same people would be coming to that meeting. In the meantime, I came across an article written by the president of that very bank which specifically stated they were being very lenient with those who held mortgages with them because of the economic downturn. He emphasized they were willing to help them get through this challenging time. God gave me wisdom to pull out the article in the middle of the meeting.

I said, "If you don't mind, I am going to read this article to you; then, I have a question." After reading, I gave them the name of the author. "This is your president. My question: Is he lying? It appears to me that you are telling me something that is completely opposite of what he just said. Therefore, I am requesting a face-to-face meeting with him, so we can determine whether he meant what he wrote."

They looked somewhat stunned. To make a long story short, the local president of the bank took back our loans, and we were back in line with the technical component. Did I say that the covenant was challenging? That was a big challenge. However, I knew God was in control, and somehow we would weather the storm. Eventually, the bank gave us even more favorable terms than what we had, and we now have one of the lowest interest rates in the country as a church. Covenant was challenged and covenant came through. Though the bank might have been good with its numbers, it didn't understand the covenant Shirley and I lived by, which said **One** + **One** = **One**. We knew we were on the Lord's side, and they didn't have a chance. God's math is always preferable to the bank's. When you live in covenant and it is challenged, you discover He is the God of more than enough. Covenant living never diminishes you, it only increases you.

Not only were we challenged in the financial aspect of the ministry, Shirley and I realized we needed to change the way we were doing church. We always had great weekend services and results. Our concern was raising up leaders who would take the ministry to the next level. It seemed as if we had become stagnant and needed a new direction. During this time, we had to ask and answer some very difficult questions.

You must learn to live the questions, not just the answers.

You must learn to live the questions, not just the answers.

We are often more energetic and more aggressive, more motivated about things we don't know than the truths and knowledge we possess. What you know can often lose its effectiveness the longer you live that knowledge. It no longer propels us forward. Questions can send us searching, longing, looking, demanding, and expecting answers. In the process, our minds are expanded, our knowledge is enlarged, our spirits are energized, and we experience increase. A fear of the unknown will often enrich your life when you confront it. Learn never to fear your times of questioning.

As you read the Bible, you find God challenging His people with new experiences, new places, new battles, new victories. For sure, we had many, many questions coming out of obtaining a new facility and the dramatic downturn of the economy. Often God does not answer some of our questions because we are not ready for His answer. How could He perform such great miracles to purchase this new facility knowing the economic challenge was coming? Thus, He taught us to live everything, especially our questions, knowing all the while, nothing takes Him by surprise. Once God spoke to me when I was demanding an answer in a stressful situation:

"You cannot hear the answer I am giving because you are so focused on the answer you want." How often have you been so focused on an answer you desired, that you couldn't hear the one God was giving you? In this instance, I was guilty as charged.

In the Old Testament, Moses was disillusioned and wondered why God had instructed him to lead Israel to the Promised Land. Listen to his complaint:

The [Israeli] foremen said to Moses and Aaron, "May the Lord judge and punish you for making us stink before Pharaoh and his officials. You have put a sword into their hands, an excuse to kill us! (Exodus 5:21 NLT).

Out of our challenges, we learned what Moses learned: Sometimes when you do exactly as God has instructed, things get worse, at least from *your* perspective. We learned something during this time concerning doing God's will—discouragement with present challenges is not the same as disobedience. Anytime there is a huge challenge that appears negative on the surface, God is not looking to just fix the problem. He wants you to be increased by His answer. With every challenge, God is looking to increase our value in His Kingdom.

Sometimes, we only have one piece of the puzzle, but God sees the whole picture. The answer God has for you is bigger than you, more than you, and greater than you could ever think, dream, or envision it to be. Remember, He is the God of the impossible.

"God can make even your enemies be at peace with you" (Proverbs 16:7).

> **"God can make even your enemies be at peace with you" (Proverbs 16:7).**

God's answers are always bigger than your questions. The question marks of life can often be our most profitable experiences. When we are filled with answers, we get lazy, sluggish, and even bored. Living full of questions gets us out of our mundane routines, to go where we haven't been, to do what we haven't done, all the while seeking answers. There is a huge difference between what God is doing and what you actually see Him doing. It's almost like an iceberg—only a very small part is seen above the water while the vast majority of it is below the surface.

Shirley and I often felt our challenges were really large because we only saw the challenge and weren't able to discern what God was doing, nor were we able to figure out what He was going to do. During that time, she had far more faith than me. When I observed how much faith she had in those moments, I was very envious. No question about it—she was the strongest of the two of us when we lacked answers to pressing questions. When we looked at our ministry programs and questioned what we were doing and why we were doing it, we noticed some weak links. Even though we didn't want to admit it, we were getting older. Serious questions began to arise in our lives. By this time, the who, what, why questions have pretty much been answered. We have lived our destiny and have seen it fully activated over the course of our ministry.

The big question now is: Who takes over when we are no longer here? That drove us to make some very positive changes in the way we were doing leadership training. As I sought the Lord about this, I felt led to begin an internship class that would consist of training young people for ministry. Shirley loved young people and was always able to bond with them. Together we wanted them to see the power of God's covenant love in and through us.

It wasn't like we needed something else to do, but Tony felt very strongly about this class. He devised a very disciplined format—meeting for 90 minutes on a Monday night for nine months. In the first class, we handpicked those who would be a part. There were 37 students along with Tony and me, and a dear friend in ministry, Steve Korn. Tony began to write the curriculum as we taught the classes, and eventually we determined there would be five blocks of material—discipline, identity, leadership, purpose, and covenant. At the time, it seemed we over obligated ourselves in trying to pull this off. As we got into the class, I interjected some wisdom from our years of ministry and practical things to go along with his biblical teaching. Once again, it was our principle of One + One = One. It seemed like God used that principle of oneness to speak into the hearts of those young people—letting them see our love for each other and our love for them.

Over the next 12 years, over 250 people would go through the class. What a great thrill it was to see some of them meet their spouse while in the class. Those weddings were very special for me and Tony, knowing we had a small part to play in them coming together. Even to this day, the internship is paying big dividends because many of them serve in a leadership capacity in the church and in this community. Our current youth minister was in that first class, and so was a young lady who helped write this book with

Tony, Lauren Clark. (You should also read *The Diamond Life: You Are More Than Have Become*, which she helped Tony write.)

Out of the challenging questions we asked, several new ministries were birthed. I always wanted to bring the women together with a Saturday morning brunch once per quarter, as well as conduct a Friday night worship service. Our worship services were very powerful for the ladies, and God performed many miracles of deliverance as we prayed and sought Him together. The brunch was a wonderful time of fellowship and allowed us to get to know each other in a more intimate setting. I continued both of these ministries right up through 2020. Though I was not physically well during three of those years, I never missed one of those meetings. God's grace was truly sufficient for me, knowing I wanted to be there.

During this season of physical challenge, my daughter, Melony, was right by my side helping to organize and facilitate both of these ministries. What a godsend she has been. She is so gifted in administration, organization, and all the little details needed to be carried out to make ministry work. Her heart is ever turned toward God to do whatever He needs done in His Kingdom work here. While I was doing this, Tony was very energized in gathering men for the REAL Men ministry.

For many years, I taught men eight weeks at a time, three times a year in a classroom setting. Hundreds of men came through those classes. It had been many years since those classes ended, and I had a strong desire to teach the men again. We changed the venue to the restaurant in our new church building and made it a Saturday morning breakfast. Between 75 to 100 men show up to fellowship and learn the truths of God's Word about living a godly life and serving Him in His Kingdom. These are special times of developing spiritual intimacy. Often men bring friends who do not attend the church, and many of them become regulars. It is such a privilege to help these men grow into REAL Men for His Kingdom.

One young man drove from Detroit and was on the management team for General Motors. He told me the teaching had transformed his life, and he was able to share some of the concepts he was learning with team members from work. Many of the men that are regulars in that class have taken on positions of leadership in the church. Three of the men were ordained into ministry. Time and again, we would hear testimonies of how God was healing a marriage or a family through these Saturday morning sessions. There is no greater joy in ministry than knowing what you are doing is making a difference in someone's life. So many times, men come to breakfast with questions about marriage, work, profession, fatherhood, business, and God provides answers. One man told me he had been to many high-level conferences where business principles were taught. He shared with me what he was getting in the REAL Men breakfasts far exceeded the expensive conferences. One young man said he spent $65,000 on a college education, but he got more from the internship class and the REAL Men ministry than college.

The teaching is always built around a covenant with God and a covenant with each other. For many of these men, it was the first time they had heard this message. Perhaps these ministries would not have been birthed without the great challenges we faced during these years.

For more than 20 years, God had spoken to me about the "diamond formula" and how a diamond is made. The highest quality diamonds come from deep in the heart of the Earth, over 5,000 degrees of heat, a million pounds of pressure per square inch, and millions of years. It became a diamond with heat, pressure, and time. It seemed that this formula would never leave my mind. And the book *The Diamond Life: You Are More Than You Have Become* was written. The book became a huge success and was sold in several countries. A businessman on the West Coast, who had more than 20,000 people in his network marketing business, said it was one of the best books he ever read. They ordered several thousand copies for their associates. When you stop to think about it, the challenge really is about making diamonds of us all. We all face those moments of heat, pressure, and time in the process of living our lives. Covenant is challenging, but covenant is rewarding. Although Shirley and I had been in ministry for four decades, we were still learning we are more than we have become. What we didn't know at this time was that our greatest challenges lay ahead of us. Everything we had learned about God and covenant was going to be put to the test in a life or death situation we would soon face.

In 2016, Shirley began to lose weight and found difficulty digesting her food. At first, we thought it was acid reflux but later would be told it was the narrowing of her esophagus. Over the next two years, we would learn she was misdiagnosed. After her esophagus would be stretched, she could eat for a few weeks, then it would close back up again.

Her heart's desire was to take her grandchildren to the Holy Land and even though she struggled physically, in November 2016, we traveled with them there. Our daughter and son-in-law joined Perry Stone there. Every day, her face, her smile, her joy radiated to everyone her delight in having her granddaughters and daughter see the Holy Land and experience so many of the things in the Bible. This was one of her life's greatest highlights.

Daily, I would find soft foods for her to eat to keep her energy up during the trip. Using natural peanut butter, I would mix it with bananas for her to eat. She never missed a day, an event, a place, an excursion, the whole time. I always marveled at who she was—she was truly more than I could

Abe Lincoln once said, "It is not the years in your life that count, it is the life in your years."

ever describe in words. Her love for God, her love of life, and her love of family were infectious. She would always say, "I'm so glad we went to Israel with our children and grandchildren."

In spite of these challenges and the ones we would face in the near future, we discovered great joy in the secret of covenant living.

Abe Lincoln once said, "It is not the years in your life that count, it is the life in your years."

Your life should be filled with dreams. Dreams come day by day. You have to allow time for your dream. You have to allow God time to breathe the dream into you. When you have a God-dream, it ignores obstacles. Don't get caught up in the ordinary—rise to the extraordinary! Wherever He is calling you, He is already there. Wake up, stand up, take ground, and take it fast! It is not the dream of a lifetime, but the dream that takes a lifetime.

We had to trust God enough to know that He would bring the dream of our hearts to pass if we were only prepared to wait for His timing. What a feeling to know that you are in the right place at the right time, doing what you are supposed to be doing. God told us, "I am going to give you the dream of your heart," and He will do the same for you. Be faithful and persistent to do what God tells you to do. Just rejoice and have a good time because it is on the way! Anything is possible when you believe. Always add your faith to your dream, knowing faith is an action word.

In God's Word, faith and obedience cannot be separated. What you truly believe, you are motivated to do. One of life's difficult truths is that every season has fruit—even a winter season. In our seasons of life, God is trying to teach me about me—and teach you about you. Some suggest God permits a season to see how you will respond. Nothing could be further from the truth since He already knows everything, including your response. You don't really invite a season of life—they come without invitation. Never compare seasons—you may be in winter while your friend is in fall harvest. Seasons also have no respect for your opinions. One day you wake up and you're in a season of grief or mourning, of financial stress, or marital difficulties. God wants you to embrace your seasons because, in the midst of your season, He is trying to season you. Shirley and I were going to face the most difficult season of our life, in which we would learn that life really isn't fair. Yet, everything we had learned about oneness with God and with each other would bring miraculous support to the months and years of great physical challenge for her. We weathered this season because we were one with God and one with each other. Oneness in a marriage can often balance the seasons of unfairness. Even when life isn't fair, God is always just.

Oneisms from Chapter 8

- Nothing gets into your life without coming through His hands.
- Whatever He permits in your life is meant to increase you, not diminish you.
- The dark places of life must become for us the birthplace of vision.
- You must learn to live the questions, not just the answers. We are often more energetic and more aggressive, more motivated about things we don't know than the truths and knowledge we do know.
- Anytime there is a huge challenge that appears negative on the surface, God is not looking to just fix the problem. He wants you to be increased by His answer.
- God created you to live your covenant with Him.
- Always remember, you are more than you have become.
- God wants you to embrace your seasons because, in the midst of your season, He is trying to season you.

Chapter 9

When Life Isn't Fair

WITHIN each of us, there are desires for life's circumstances to be fair. Your success as a person in charge of your own life begins the moment you plan a strategy to meet and overcome the forces that oppose you. Without question, this attack on my physical body had begun to take a toll on my life. Tony and I had always been very healthy, full of energy, and loved living life. By this time, I had already dropped 25 pounds and suffered a severe loss of energy. In spite of all this, we were determined to find an answer and overcome something we considered to be a temporary setback.

What life dishes out is not always God. Life's circumstances and God are not the same things. Being someone who loved organization and working with details, I knew we needed a plan. The internet became a great friend as I researched the symptoms I was having. When life isn't fair, you get pushed out of your comfort zone. Unfairness demands you have an unwavering faith you can and will prevail, regardless of your current challenges. Some of the things I learned in my research led me to have the discipline to confront the most brutal facts of my symptoms. By the middle of 2017, Tony was getting very concerned about my condition and wanted me to see a specialist. Whether it was fear or denial, I knew things had to change. Tony even scheduled an appointment in Ann Arbor, but I canceled it.

God had given me a tremendous tolerance for pain through-out my life. Someone once said, "Pain is inevitable, and suffering is optional." While I knew we had to do something different than what we were doing, I wasn't sure what was required of me. Satan wants to ruin our testimony, rob us, and cause us to wallow in self-pity. Feeling sorry for myself was not something I ever felt comfortable with.

> The human spirit grows strong by challenge and resistance.

The human spirit grows strong by challenge and resistance.

Extraordinary things can be accomplished by ordinary people who simply refuse to allow their struggle to define them. This physical infirmity wasn't going to define me.

In one of his messages, Tony used this quote which spoke to me:

> *Never be bullied into silence.*
> *Never allow yourself to be made a victim.*
>
> *Accept no one's definition of your life but define yourself.*
> *—Harvey Firestone*

Every attack of the enemy is intended to diminish who and what you are. Tony had taught me so much about life, its unfairness, its challenges, and how we are to respond to them. It's not what happens to you, but what happens within you that really matters.

Often when he was counseling people through difficult times, especially illness and disease, he would talk about statistical probabilities. This really helped me, and perhaps it will speak to you. Throughout life, anyone's life, there will be people who get killed in an accident of some kind, an automobile crash, an airplane crash, or they die from disease or some other cause of death. Statistical probabilities—these things continually happen, day in and day out, all over the world. They aren't fair, but they happen.

From him, I learned so many things about how to live life. One of his favorites verses is:

I Corinthians 10:13 (MSG) — No test or temptation that comes your way is beyond the course of what others have had to face. All you need to remember is that God will never let you down; He'll never let you be pushed past your limit; He'll always be there to help you come through it.

All during this time, we were praying and believing together for a divine miracle of healing. However, my condition continued to worsen throughout 2017. Tony brought me a research document stating my symptoms could possibly be cancer. The document came from a medical website, but I wasn't ready to hear that. Despite his insistence that we see a specialist, I continued to pray and believe for a miracle and continued to have my esophagus stretched. Eventually, I came to realize we had to do something different. There was a specialist at the clinic who admitted me to the hospital, so he could go down my esophagus and stomach to get a look.

When I awoke from his examination, he shared with us he had found a tumor at the gastroesophageal junction, GEJ. He took a biopsy of it and sent it off to the lab. The results came back; it was cancerous. Tears began to flow down my face. Tony, Melony, and I were shocked at the report. How could this be? Fear came over me. Fear of dying. Tony took my hand and encouraged me with God's Truth—"We will fight this, and we will beat it. We will get a miracle."

I don't remember much about the next few days. My body was frail from loss of weight, and I was unable to eat much. Questions filled my mind. We faced some major decisions. Where would I go to get treatment and which doctor would perform it?

Before I share that with you, let's go back to a story 30 years ago which took place at our church. At the close of a Sunday night service, Tony invited people to the altar who wanted to know their God-called purpose in life. A young mother, Pam Schlembach, came forward as Tony took hold of her hands. His words were rather profound as he spoke of the healing in them. Pam was a nurse but had always dreamed of becoming a doctor. With a husband and two small children, she was concerned about what such a time commitment would do to her family. After the service, she shared with us how she had asked God for Tony to pray over her as a sign she was to pursue this career path. After graduating from University of Toledo Medical Center hospital, she was hired by MD Anderson in Houston, Texas, as a radiation oncologist. Today, she is the director of their clinic in the Woodlands. Who knew at that time in 2018, I would need her to use those healing hands to treat me? Obviously, God knew.

During your lifetime, you encounter two different kinds of friends—friends of the road and friends of the heart. Friends of the road come into your life for a season and are then gone. Friends of the heart remain there forever; they are covenant friends. Such were Chuck and Pam to us.

I remember hearing the statement—God is preparing you for what He has prepared for you. Pam, along with her husband, Chuck, opened their home for us to stay in while I was being treated at the clinic. She chose the best doctors for my chemo and surgery, and of course, we knew she was the best for the radiation. Dr. Kovitz managed the chemo treatments, and Dr. Swisher, chief of surgery, operated on me. From our very first visit to Houston, Tony and I felt peace about being there. Later, I called Melony to let her know we felt peace and knew this was where we needed to be. She told me the prayer team of the church had just been praying we would feel peace about Houston.

In early March, we flew to Houston to begin my treatments and have a feeding tube inserted. By then, I had lost almost 50 pounds and my body desperately needed nourishment. We would stay with Chuck and Pam from Sunday evening until Friday and then fly home to Toledo. During the six weeks of radiation and chemo, I was able to go home on the weekends each time. Being in the church and experiencing His supernatural Presence kept me going.

We stayed on the second floor of their home, which sits on a beautiful lake. Our room had a balcony, and often we would sit there to watch the sun go down on the lake. They were so kind and gracious to us. In the afternoons, I would take a nap, being exhausted from my morning treatments. Tony would get up early every morning to pray and then do my feeding through the tube because it had to be three hours prior to the treatments. One day, I woke up from my afternoon nap and decided to walk out onto the balcony. There I saw him stretched out in the chair sound asleep. I got my phone and took his picture and put it on Facebook. When he woke up, I showed it to him, and he said, "No, you really didn't do that!" No husband could have taken better care of me, and I often told him that.

I'm not sure anyone can prepare for cancer or the effects the treatments have on a body. The experience of weakness, coughing, fatigue, hoarseness, bone pain, loss of hair, eyebrows, and eyelashes, nausea, headaches, nose bleeds, and a runny nose were at times severe. Frequently, it was just more than I could take. Our faith got us through. We were always convinced God would not allow more on us than we could handle. After six weeks of treatments of chemo and radiation in Houston, we arrived back home in May 2018. Tony and I were determined to take our life back and return to some form of normalcy. When life isn't fair, you cannot afford to lose your

> You will never climb beyond the limitations of your personal belief system.

God-perspective. Life should never be empowered to make us victims. I was made to be a victor.

You will never climb beyond the limitations of your personal belief system.

Throughout the summer months, many people were praying for me—our church family and friends, our Church of God family—all in agreement against this vicious attack on my life. There were many words of encouragement and much comfort from thousands of people. I felt privileged that I didn't have to go through this without my church family. Anyone facing a battle of cancer needs all the support and prayer you can get to walk this path of cancer.

Tony and I have always led healthy lives, worked hard, and stayed busy because of our love for the ministry. From the time I was a child, I knew God wanted me to serve Him in His Kingdom. I am so grateful for every day God has given me. Now I view people so differently. My love for people is felt more deeply today, especially those I see struggling with sickness and disease.

We have often experienced divine assignments and divine alignments with people in our lives. These people have truly touched my heart and blessed me immensely.

- While in the hospital and recovering from my surgeries, Brian and Michelle Lawhon drove from Austin to Houston at God's direction to pray for me. That prayer time in my hospital room was powerful. Michelle was suffering herself, and we all began to pray for healing for both of us.

- Floyd and Gay Lawhon, close friends since our days at Lee University, called and prayed with Tony regularly to encourage him.

- Carl and Diane Malz, friends and intercessors for more than 40 years, prayed and sent encouraging words on a weekly basis.

- Mario and Michelle Murillo called and prayed often with me as I would go into treatment, not knowing that was the exact time I needed them.

- Andric Daugherty, the associate pastor from Pathway Church, was in Houston visiting another member found out we were in the same hospital.

- People like Carmen Rocha flew from California to pray with me and anoint us.

- Isabelle Rocha joined her sister, Carmen, even during the coronavirus outbreak. It was such an act of faith to even get on a plane.

- Dennis Watkins, who leads our prayer ministry at General Headquarters, prayed for us regularly.

- Bishop Tim Hill and the Executive Committee and Executive Council of the Church of God called and prayed with us.

- Our overseer "Bishop Martin" and his wife, Rosalyn, came to theChurch several times to pray for me.

- Perry and Pam Stone prayed for me on the phone during his weekly Thursday night prayer services.

- Our church elders, Cedric and Brenda Franklin, often sent prayers by text.

- Our prayer leaders, Don and Lori Weier, came to my home to pray with me.

- Our church elders, Dr. Mark and Nancy Neumann, came to pray with me often and check my health.

- Our church elders, Henk and Carmen Wigmans, blessed me with a beautiful wig after chemo.

- Our church elders, John and Lisa Harris, were with me in Houston and prayed with me daily.

- Our church elders, J.B. and Roxanne Burton, prayed over me constantly.

- Our church elders, Ron and Denise Dean, covered me in prayers continuously.

- Nancy Breon, a church member, rebuked the cancer at the root.

- Jane Weasel, one of our best intercessors, was always praying and encouraging me to "March forth!"

- Peggy Otieno, a ministry staff member and a dear friend, has served in ministry with us for many years and was always praying.

- Linda Greene, a friend and intercessor, came to Houston to be with me.

These are just a few of the thousands of people who stood in prayer with me and Tony during this time. Our wonderful church family held our hands, prayed for us, and were there every step of the journey—what great men and women of God.

Before my surgery in August 2018, I attended the Church of God International General Assembly in Orlando, Florida. I had never missed one since I was a little girl. At the convention, Jentezen Franklin and his wife, mother, and mother-in-law, along with John and Debbie Childers, prayed over me. One night, we rode in the van to the center with Dennis and DeRosa McGuire. Dennis always makes me laugh. The fellowship there was very rich and encouraging.

During our many decades of ministry, I never had a minister's license. Since my dad had no son, there was no one to carry on their legacy. As I prayed about it, God spoke to me about getting ordained and listing my name as Shirley Lesley Scott to honor my dad and his legacy. I felt such peace about it. After speaking to Bishop Hill and Dr. Raymond Culpepper, they approved the ordination in February 2018. Tony and I will always be grateful to the Church of God for the role they have played in our lives. We love the church very much! While I didn't do anything I wasn't already doing, I now had the papers to prove I was ordained. My grand-daughters and other women I have mentored can carry this legacy on, if God so desires. Our family is now in its fourth generation of Church of God believers. To God be the glory!

When cancer strikes, you are faced with a choice as to how you will fight the battle. It was always my intent to be a victor, not a victim. Weariness and exhaustion, weakness and nausea, along with many other symptoms have to be dealt with continuously. Tony was always there beside me, holding my hand, along with Melony, to encourage me when I would get down.

When life is unfair, we often feel conflicted. Many days, I would ask God why I was having to go through this, but I never received that answer. Life really is not fair. Sometimes you will suffer without a reason why. During those times, I learned to throw myself fully and completely on the mercy and the care of God. A passage of Scripture in 1 Peter 5:7 (AMPC) gave me comfort:

Casting the whole of your care [all your anxieties,
all your worries, all your concerns, once and for all]
on Him, for He cares for you affectionately
and cares about you watchfully.

Life is not always fair. Sometimes it can even be brutal. My desire is to never have a pity party. With all of my heart, I want to be an example of someone who stood strong under the attack of the enemy and show others what living by faith really means. Within each of us, there is a desire for circumstances to be fair. Tony and I never wanted to feel sorry for ourselves regardless of what life dealt us. We also never wanted to be angry about our difficulties. Circumstances in life should never define who you are, and that includes cancer. God's Word teaches us the human spirit grows strong by challenge and resistance. Through many decades of ministry, Tony has thoroughly researched God's Word to dig out principles of life that work in spite of troublesome times. Being a wordsmith, he loves word studies in the Bible and makes certain portions of Scripture come alive by focusing on their meaning. I have always loved that about his teaching.

In Isaiah 40:1, God commands him to comfort His people:

"Comfort, O comfort My people," says your God.

Comfort means "to give breath to" or "to give breath to again." When life is unfair, when it takes the breath out of you, God puts breath back into you.

In Isaiah 40:28-31, God gives power to the weak and increases strength to those who have no might.

The word "increase" means to project "similar to when one shoots an arrow." When God sees one of His children in this kind of condition, He sends an arrow of energy into their spirit to instantly revive their hope. The Word of God is very clear to those of us who know Him. He simply says, "Faint not!" When you're battling cancer and striving to live, there are good days when hope rises and challenging days when it is difficult to go on. No one expects to grow up and live with cancer.

What do we want to be when we grow up? From early childhood, we remember pondering the answer to that question. Looking back now, we realize that question is still being answered. Truly life is an ongoing process where we start out doing, move on to becoming, and hopefully end up feeling fulfilled. Realizing we are today the sum total of all our choices and decisions, the responsibility for what we have become is solely ours.

How is it possible to plan a successful life? What is the standard of measurement one should use? Perhaps the apostle Paul says it best in Ephesians 4:13 (AMPC):

[That it might develop] until we all attain oneness in the faith and in the comprehension of the [full and accurate] knowledge of the Son of God, that [we might arrive] at really mature manhood (the completeness of personality which is nothing less than the standard height of Christ's own perfection), the measure of the stature of the fullness of the Christ and the completeness found in Him.

Many days, I was faint, and I was weary. Even in unfairness, God has a plan, a strategy to bless us. When we determine how we handle our circumstances, He becomes the wind in our sails. He puts breath back into us when life takes our breath away.

Ella Wheeler Wilcox wrote this timely poem:

> One ship sails east and another west,
> By the self-same winds that blow;
> 'Tis the set of the sails and not the gails,
> that tells the way we go.
>
> Like the winds of the sea
> Are the waves of time,
> As we journey along through life;
> 'Tis the set of the soul,
> That determines the goal
> And not the calm or the strife.

Unfairness, disappointment, and failure should never be permitted to establish the boundaries of our life. Our covenant of faith in God was about to be stretched like never before. There is nothing in life that prepares you for something like this. My life had never been threatened before, and I was determined to find an answer. Calling upon the Word of God in me and all the faith I could muster, I would strive to live.

Oneisms from Chapter 9

- Extraordinary things can be accomplished by ordinary people who simply refuse to allow their struggle to define them.
- Every attack of the enemy is used to diminish who and what you are.
- God is preparing you for what He has prepared for you.
- Always remember: God will not allow more on you than you can handle.
- Be a victor, not a victim.
- Life really is not fair. Sometimes you will suffer without a reason why. During those times, throw yourself fully and completely on the mercy and the care of God.
- Life's circumstances should never define who you are.
- You decide what in life defines you.

Part 4:

When the Answers Don't Come

Chapter 10

Striving to Live

WHAT a powerful truth—we as individuals can author, define, the story of our lives. While circumstances can often **reveal who you are**, they should never **define who you are**. As a woman, wife, mom, servant, and pastor, I refuse to be defined as someone with cancer. Let me make this clear to you—never will I give in to this sickness, because I will live every day to the fullest and leave a legacy to all who know me. I will fight the good fight of faith to the very end of my life and enter into the Presence of God hearing Him say, "Well done, you good and faithful servant."

Scripture is very clear that sometimes we have to go through hard times so on our journey we can minister to others who are going through similar trials.

> I Corinthians 1:4 (TPT) says, He always comes
> alongside us to comfort us in every suffering so
> that we can come alongside those who are in
> any painful trial. We can bring them this same
> comfort that God has poured out upon us.

I understand now more than ever what I am to do and have already ministered to many women. The following is a Word that was spoken over me years ago by Lee Grady from *Charisma Magazine*.

February 8, 2004

"And I just speak over my sister now. Thank You, Lord, for the new season that You are bringing her into. Thank You for the compassion that is deepening. And, Lord, I see such practical training flowing out of her and being imparted into others. But, Lord, I also see many leaders coming and people who have been pent up and have been bottled up for years. They've never been able to say what was really going on inside of them. And this precious vessel is going to be the one who's going to uncork them. And the pain is going to flow out, and Lord, she's going to be a minister of healing to those who have been sidelined by disappointment, sidelined by the devil's onslaught, sidelined by the actions of Christian people. And, Lord, there's a deep, deep anointing of emotional healing that's resting upon this one. And I just say an increase now in Jesus' name. Lord, there's an anointing to pull the spears out of the backs of people who have been stabbed and wounded in battle. I see many, many women in ministry coming to her. Some of them are wives, and they are devastated. It's almost like they are beyond hope. But I say, Lord, this one will be able to bring them out of the ICU and bring them into a place of recovery. The enemy's intention was for those people to just die and never recover what they lost. But because of this woman, she is an intervener for Jesus, and I say right now she's going to intervene in some very strategic situations. And because of the intervention, churches and ministries will get right back on track instead of being derailed, says the Lord."

Over the last two years (2016-2017), I had lost 50 pounds and had a feeding tube for the last seven months. Nothing kept me from church or church activities, always making sure the feeding tube was hidden. It was never in my character to feel sorry for myself, knowing God had me and would take care of me. For months, I continued to build up my faith and trust in Him daily. His Word heals. All of our extended family: Doris, Joyce, Don, Carol, Kim, Shani, Leianne, Melissa, Scott, Drew, and Mikel Ann, plus all the people who loved me from my church family and my city were praying for me daily.

After attending the General Assembly, we traveled back to Houston for my surgery to remove the tumor. Accompanying us on this trip was my son, Darin, and my daughter, Melony, my sister, Sharon, (who had just gone through breast cancer treatment and is in remission now) and our elders Jon and Lisa Harris. We all stayed together at a great hotel the night before and had a very nice meal together. Of course, I still was not eating, and I know it was hard for them to eat with me there, but not for me. We had a great time together.

Early the next morning, we all met in the hotel lobby to go over to the hospital for surgery. All of us were crying, but mostly we were confident I was going to be alright. Arriving at the hospital, they immediately began to prep me for surgery, and then we all gathered, prayed, and said our goodbyes.

I have always believed if you love every day and say the things you need to say to people, then there is no unforgiveness or anything you must make right with anyone. Daily, I had practiced this. Our spirit tells us if we need to apologize, then say, "I'm sorry." Stress comes from fear, anger, bitterness, unforgiveness, jealousy, regret, worry, and anxiety. Regularly, I kept my spirit free of any distractions, so I could worship God with my whole heart. After 46 years of pastoring, there are a lot of hurts, disappointments, misunderstandings, and rejections because we are all human. People are always coming and going out of our lives, especially in church ministry, but we must learn not to take it personally. You can't carry that load. You have to accept the choices people make. You must keep loving no matter what. Is that hard sometimes? Yes, it is, but it is possible! Try to always end with people like you started with them—love and sweet departures.

As I entered for surgery, the song lyrics I kept singing in my head were: "I'm no longer a slave to fear, I am a child of God." Nothing was going to hinder or diminish my faith, especially not fear. Going into surgery, I would always close my eyes and say His name—Jesus—over and over. Peace would flood me and keep me as Isaiah 26:3 says,

> You will keep in perfect and constant peace the one whose mind is steadfast [that is, committed and focused on You—in both inclination and character], because he trusts and takes refuge in You [with hope and confident expectation].

Psalm 34:1-4 (AMPC) has also ministered to me often.

> I will bless the Lord at all times; His praise shall continually be in my mouth. My soul makes its boast in the Lord; the humble and downtrodden will hear it and rejoice. O magnify the Lord with me, and let us lift up His name together. I sought the Lord [on the authority of His Word], and He answered me, and delivered me from all my fears.

Not knowing what to expect from the surgery, I was almost in shock when I woke up seven hours later. There were machines and tubes everywhere, which can be pretty scary if you don't have the peace of God surrounding you. Nurses were coming in and saying how well I did in the surgery, and I was going to be fine. The first few days were rough, but Tony and Melony would take me outside in a wheelchair every day with all the equipment to get some fresh air and sun on my face. This was healing also! Some days I didn't think I could do it, but they insisted. How thankful I am for the push. After 14 days in the hospital, I was longing to go home. But because of a leak in my esophagus from the surgery, they had to go in and repair it. And as a result of this, it doubled my hospital stay and recovery. Keeping my mind on Jesus, I refused to be discouraged, though I was disappointed. Dr. Swisher said I was the strongest person he had ever met, but I assured him it was the God in me. This made my spirit strong. We ministered to the doctor many times over these days. Tony was preaching on the subject, "The Secret Place," and Dr. Swisher loved to hear about his sermons on Monday when we met with him. He told him "The Secret Place" is a couch where you meditate on Jesus. He encouraged the doctor to practice His peace.

When going down for the second surgery, a chaplain came by the holding room to pray with me. We found out he was from Nigeria and was Pentecostal. We all began to pray in the Spirit—what a happening—all God! These little, yet divine, moments truly lifted my spirits.

Two major surgeries in two weeks are a lot. My daughter, Melony, sat in a chair by my bed, day and night, for 14 days making sure I was alright. She checked every pill and every shot the nurses gave me; she took such good care of me. The nurses and Dr. Swisher told her she would have been an excellent nurse!

For three weeks, Tony flew home for weekend services in Toledo and flew back on Sunday evening to Houston. He slept in a recliner on the other side of my bed! These two provided such love, such compassion, always putting me first.

Back in 2006, Dave and Melony moved into a condo adjoined to ours, and we have taken care of each other since then. It's like the olden days when you have dinner together and your grandkids come over anytime. This has been a great joy to us. God has blessed us so much. She serves as the Executive Pastor of the ministry where we daily serve together as a family. She truly is a blessing to us and to everyone she is involved with. My son, Darin, and his family, who live in Nashville, check on me often and are always willing to do anything they can to help us. I am so grateful for my family.

While in Houston, everyone at church would call or text Melony and say, "Your dad is preaching and teaching the best messages ever even during this severe trial." That is really something to say after 46 years as their pastor and the thousands of messages he's written! We always listened online too, and we knew it! Only one answer...God!

He was also mad at the devil for attacking me and he declared, "He will pay big time!"

Just like I said, "God is with and in you every step of the way." I felt like I was in a bubble protected by the Holy Spirit in spite of my circumstances.

I remember the day they said I could have some chicken broth—it had been months since I had real food! Tony went to a famous restaurant to get chicken noodle soup for me because he didn't want me to eat hospital food. To this day, I remember the first taste. It was as delicious as a filet! Even though I still had the feeding tube, I was still thankful I could begin eating some real food. This was a miracle!

Finally, on the 28th of August 2018, I was released from the hospital. We went across the street to spend the night at the hotel. Since I was too sick to fly commercial, Perry Stone sent his private jet to pick us up. This was on Wednesday, the 19th of August. I was able to lay down in my seat with Tony and Melony on board with me. We flew into the Toledo Express Airport where an ambulance was waiting to transport me home. A great multitude of people from the church was there to welcome me home with signs, flowers, and balloons. Their expressions of love brought tears to my eyes. Many of them followed us to our home, and after I was taken into my bedroom, they gathered around me to rejoice and pray. All of us were expecting a great miracle. While I was recovering from the surgeries, some nurses from theChurch would come and sit with me to monitor my progress. Many would come simply to pray over me. What great comfort from God's people. In spite of the pain, I was determined to get off the pain medications as quickly as possible.

During our entire 46 years of ministry in Toledo, there was hardly ever a time I missed the weekend services. As I recovered at home, I was watching a service online and felt the Holy Spirit say, "Get up and get dressed and go to the church; take your seat back."

Only in the strength of the Holy Spirit could I have done that. Melony came to pick me up, and I well remember the look on Tony's face when he saw me walk in. Since that time, I have not missed a service or given up my seat.

Thanksgiving and Christmas are my two favorite holidays. Our family always gathers during those times for great food and fellowship. After two years of not being able to eat much, I can tell you I looked forward to those meals. Tony and I enjoyed cooking together. When we sat down to eat our Thanksgiving dinner, Tony began to weep and thank God for His blessings to us as a family. It was a very touching moment for me with our family all there. All of us were crying. For us as a family, it was a very special moment of thanksgiving for His goodness to us.

Christmas decorations have always been exciting to me. I love the lights, the tree, the wreaths, and the decorations on the mantle. This Christmas of 2018 was very special. While we didn't get together that often during the year, these holidays were always mandatory for us. In my life, I love God, I love my family, and I love His church. When the ten of us are together, there is always a lot of laughter and joy.

Month by month I was getting stronger, and my hair was growing back and getting thicker. My six-month checkup at MD Anderson was coming up in March 2019. Once again, we flew out on Sunday afternoon to do a PET scan on Monday. We were anxious when we met with Dr. Swisher to see the results. The news could not have been better. They found no cancer! You can't imagine the relief I felt from this report. We came home and shared the good news with the church on the weekend. We had a joyous time of celebration. Although we knew the battle for my life would continue, slowly but surely, we were going to take back what the enemy had stolen from us. During that summer, I noticed that my energy was coming back, and I was sleeping much better. There was a look on Tony's face of great relief as we both believed God was giving us a miracle. I always knew Tony would have a difficult time if anything happened to me. He would always say, "I pray God takes me before He takes you because I don't want to be here without you." This was just a small step in the right direction. Dr. Swisher had told us we needed at least two years of clean scans and at least five years of being cancer-free for a full recovery. The next few months I was filled with optimism, hope, and thankfulness to God for the amazing report. Along with our church and family, we had many days, weeks, and months of joyous celebration at the goodness of God. Sometime in August, we had to plan our one-year checkup in Houston. Both of us were very anxious to get this done, believing God was healing me completely. There was some anxiety, but overall, our spirits were strong and our expectations were very high.

We flew out on Sunday afternoon in September 2019 to do the PET scan on Monday. While waiting in Dr. Swisher's office on Tuesday, the nurse came in to say there were some abnormalities he wanted to discuss with me. When he came in, he had a look on his face that said the report was not good. He proceeded to point out there were four very small spots on the scan which showed cancer did in fact return. We had to stay longer and meet with the oncologist the next day, who recommended another round of chemo. While researching esophageal cancer, I found a report that said immunotherapy had been proven to help, and the side effects were very minimal. Dr. Kovitz did not want me to have immunotherapy; he wanted another round of chemo and then a trial of immunotherapy. The thought of going into chemo treatments again was very depressing, so I insisted we speak to another oncologist who agreed to try immunotherapy for three months.

MD Anderson would oversee the immunotherapy infusions, but they would be done in Toledo. After the infusions were finished, I returned to MD Anderson for a scan which showed the immunotherapy was not effective. I was devastated, feeling in my spirit the immunotherapy was supposed to be the path forward. Afterward, we discussed a new round of very strong chemo which would be done in Toledo. A local doctor of oncology began my treatments in February 2020. For the first six weeks, the chemo sessions went well, but the side effects were harsh again. However, I was determined to do whatever it took to beat this cancer and to live.

Chemo does devastating things to one's body—food does not smell pleasant, nor does it taste good. And yet, I needed to maintain my strength. Though I began to lose weight, I tried to keep it from Tony. He obviously knew I wasn't eating much, so we discussed the possibility of going back to the feeding tube. While I didn't like the thought of that, eventually I would have no choice. The enemy was attacking my mind once again with thoughts of not living.

Although Tony and I had always been truthful and honest with each other about everything in our lives, I just didn't want to have a conversation with him about me not making it. That discussion would have been very difficult for him. Life was getting to be a great challenge, but I was striving to live.

During this time, I do not believe I ever thought of the possibility of her not making it. My faith was strong, her faith was strong, and people around the world were joining us daily in prayer. We had to win this battle for her, and very selfishly because I could never see myself without her.

As 2019 came to a close, none of us knew this would be our last Christmas together with her. Oh, God, how she loved the holidays. Having the family around us and just enjoying each other. I remember her saying something like, "We never know what the future may hold." Because we were one in spirit, soul, body, every day was important to us. Shirley was one of the most loving human beings that I have ever known. Actually, I never knew someone she didn't love. Her heart was drawn to hurting, wounded, struggling people. She simply had a gift of discernment as she would look into their eyes.

I remember her meeting a desk clerk at a local hotel where she was checking out rooms for our church guests. Afterward, she shared with me how this young lady needed someone to care about her. Not long after that, she began to attend the church, and Shirley wanted to hire her as our front desk receptionist. Today, this young lady has her own business and has an optimistic view of her future. Shirley saw that in her and helped her to realize how special she was to God. Anyone who knew Shirley knew how much she loved people. Another time, a pastor's wife drove several hours to Toledo for a Sunday night service at our church. Afterward, she shared with Shirley the struggles she was having in her role. Shirley loved on her, ministered to her, and encouraged her, and that pastor's wife has never forgotten it. The prophetic Word Lee Grady gave to Shirley was coming to pass. Whomever she came in contact with, she left her loving mark.

She loved people and loved the holidays, especially Christmas. Looking back on Christmas 2019, I don't think it could have been any more special than we made it. Looming on the horizon was the new year 2020, and things were going to get very difficult and challenging. Through it all, she was a warrior, fighting with everything in her to beat the cancer that was trying to take her life. When she had to resume the chemo treatments, I watched it take its toll on her frail body. She had gotten up to 108 pounds, and I was trying to assist her in gaining more weight. Often, I would kid her and say, "Think how blessed you are—you can eat all that you want."

During the last three and a half years, I made every effort to press into the Presence of God, to hear from Him like perhaps I have never heard before. The news of cancer returning shocked us. Though the spots were tiny, this was the one thing we didn't want to happen. Throughout my life, I have learned to be a realist, to face life as it comes, and press through no matter the circumstance. Shirley had great confidence in my relationship with God, and that meant the world to me. She was depending on me to touch the Throne of God for her. Truthfully, I felt like I had let her down, and I was disappointed in myself. She did not need to see me like that, so I remained positive in my spirit whenever I was with her. God's Word has always been the final answer for me in any given situation.

These verses sustained me during this time:

"Command you Me concerning the work of My hands" (Isaiah 45:11 NKJV).

Therefore let us [with privilege] approach the Throne of grace [that is, the Throne of God's gracious favor] with confidence *and* without fear, so that we may receive mercy [for our failures] and find [His amazing] grace to help in time of need [an appropriate blessing, coming just at the right moment] (Hebrews 4:16).

Since we have this confidence, we can also have great boldness before Him, for if we present any request agreeable to His will, He will hear us. And if we know that He hears us in whatever we ask, we also know that we have obtained the requests we ask of Him (1 John 5:14-15 TPT).

When I interpret Scripture, I do it as a literalist—I believe it means what it says. Although I knew she was struggling with the fear of dying, together we were making every effort to overcome those fears. After the six-month checkup with no cancer detected, we were on a spiritual high, believing the miracle was happening. However, the September report took the breath out of my spirit. The look in her eyes told me she would have to battle the enemy of fear, especially fear of death more so than ever before.

When Dr. Swisher gave us that report, I remember her asking him, "How much time do I have?"

Immediately I interrupted her and said, "No, no, don't ask that. I told you we are going to beat this! You are going to live; you are not going to die."

There was a war inside of my spirit. We were one, we are one, and we shall forever be one. I had loved her in life, I had loved her during this time of treatment, and I would continue to love her no matter what. No way could I see myself without her. She was going to make it, she was going to live, and God was going to be glorified.

One day, she asked, "What has God said to you about me? I know He often speaks to you about people, and He gives you a Word concerning their situations."

The question startled me, and I struggled to give her the answer. In fact, in the three years of crying out to God, there was no

Word from Him concerning our situation. But she needed to hear something, and these words came out of my mouth: *I know you will not die from this cancer, but I don't have a specific Word from God.*

For sure, it grieved my heart knowing there was no Word from Him. That didn't stop my crying out to Him. Being the priest of my family was something very serious to me. While it is true there were other things I prayed for without getting an answer, it was difficult to accept the fact no answer was coming concerning her.

Not only had our personal lives been turned upside down, but we were more spiritually conflicted than ever before in our lives. This was a season of spiritual turmoil the likes of which we had never experienced.

The year 2020 will go down in our nation's history and the world's history as perhaps the most difficult one ever. That would prove to be true for us also. Everything seemed to turn upside down.

Oneisms from Chapter 10

- 💗 Scripture is very clear that sometimes we go through hard times on our journey, so we can minister to others who are going through similar trials.

- 💗 On a daily basis, keep your spirit free of any distractions, so you can worship God with your whole heart.

- 💗 As you keep your mind on Jesus, He will keep you in perfect peace.

- 💗 Take back what the enemy has stolen.

- 💗 God expects you to remind Him of His Word.

- 💗 Regardless of your situation, never lose trust in God's Word.

Chapter 11

2020—The Upside Down Year

SOON my life and world would be turned upside down as once again there were complications in my recovery. Cancer is the worst thing that has ever happened to me, but I chose to believe that God is working this situation for my good. Even though I am afraid, I make the choice to believe. I would say, "God, I don't understand why this is happening, but I'm just going to believe that somehow You're going to work this for my good."

For the last three years, I have educated myself by researching the cancer I have. What is really surprising to me is no one in the medical field tells you very much about the effects on your body. You learn along the way and that can sometimes be very scary. I am one of those people who has never had a serious illness, or taken medications, so this is all very new to me. You go in unknowing and do what they tell you. I even had to learn that cancer shows up red in your body on scans. It would have been good to know what to expect in advance. I don't understand how the experts can find a vaccine for this coronavirus even by the end of this year when 600,000 people die each year from cancer. Where is our vaccine that could stop the spread of cancer? Surgeons remove the tumors, but often cancer cells remain in your lymph nodes or other places in the body. Surely someone could come up with a cure for cancer more effective than chemo! Billions of dollars are spent on research each year without much success. It is all so frustrating!

It's March 2020. As I am being treated with strong chemo, our nation is challenged by the coronavirus. Since I am at high risk, I had to stop being around a lot of people. My energy has taken a hit, but I keep persevering, trusting God will carry me across the finish line of victory. Cancer demands intense treatments, and you must be a fighter. Perseverance and determination are necessary to win this battle. With the world in chaos because of the coronavirus, and our lives turned upside down with my health challenge, I leaned hard on my worship life. There I continually find the strength to press on. The song "This Is How I Fight My Battles," is often on my lips. Fighting cancer demands a routine, so life can be as normal as possible. During this time, I'm still working at the church several hours of the day, even though I lay down for a while in the midst of it. Being at church and working for His Kingdom help me to focus on Him and not on my current circumstance.

Tony is very disciplined about his health and this caused me to be also. Together we have learned many things about diet, which we have implemented with a holistic approach. Before I go to chemo, I get a megadose of vitamin C by infusion. Supplements like CBD oil and mushroom beta-glucans are a part of my routine. We learned the choices we make make us. Together we settled on a mostly plant-based diet of fruits and vegetables, raw and cooked, organic if possible, and we eat a lot of baked sweet potatoes with cinnamon. Soft foods became very desirable and easier to digest. Tony would make me homemade chicken broth, mix up bananas with almond butter, yogurt, applesauce, and jello. Sometimes, he would give me a protein shake with almond milk, honey, almond butter, and Thrive mix. Pure unfiltered apple juice became my drink of choice. Always an ice cream lover, now I had to get rid of sugar in my diet. Since I was underweight and frail, I layered my clothes and used scarves to dress up my outfits. Whatever I wore, I always loved the classic look instead of the leisurely, casual wear of today. Amazingly, the body was given divine power to restore itself even after chemo treatments. And of course, I had my favorite cosmetic, the bronzer, and other facial enhancements to help.

In the two years since my treatments began, I have been able to do many things I love and enjoy. We vacationed in Hawaii with our family. Other than the Holy Land, this is my favorite place to visit in all the world. As the sun rose in the morning, we took pleasure in drinking our coffees while sitting on the beach. This time we did not do a lot of sightseeing, but just enjoyed each other's company. Hilton Hawaiian Village is our favorite place to stay. Together, we have made many memories here. For our anniversary, I wanted to go to Huntington Beach, California, with Melony, Dave, Olivia, and Mackenzie. What a beautiful time of the year and such sunrises and sunsets we got to savor. Even though I was struggling with energy, I enjoyed every day of it. This was our anniversary, and I was with the man I have loved most of my life. God made us **One + One = One.**

Because of God's goodness to us in His Kingdom, Tony is often invited to speak to ministers and spouses about our journey. During these two years, we traveled to Maryland and Alabama to share our story. We loved sharing with ministry couples. And of course, we traveled to South Carolina to be with our families at Christmas. Despite my physical challenges, I was able to do all of these things which were important to us.

Tony has always been good with words and uses special times to express his love for me. On Mother's Day 2020, he wrote this beautiful tribute. These poems, odes, always came from his heart. These were never just words to him or to me; I prefer these to cards bought at a store. Sometimes he would just write me a letter which always touched my heart.

You are the HIGHEST & BRIGHTEST STAR in my life.
Only God could create such a woman as you.
From the first moment I laid eyes on you when you were 15
until this very day—
you are the best thing that could possibly happen to me.
Because of you,
I have risen higher,
grasped more,
experienced love,
achieved success,
grown deeper,
known the most intense joy,
as together we have sought His Kingdom
power, grace, and love.
I am who I am because of your love.
You show the world how to abound and to be in want.
Your faith is a great light in a world filled with darkness.
Your suffering is producing a far greater weight of His glory.
Soon they too will see that He is a healing,
miracle-working God.
Who said...COMMAND YOU ME CONCERNING
THE WORK OF MY HANDS—Isaiah 45:11.
You are His daughter, and He is your God.
I love you, ShirleyAnn! Happy Mother's Day!

These special tributes always encouraged me. The Word of God instructs us to be encouragers. While resting at night in bed, I text other people to lift them up, especially those who are also going through difficult places in life. Each day, I speak to myself these words: I am healed, I am healthy, I am whole, in Jesus' name.

My prayer and desire are that one day soon the doctor will look at me and say, "We can find no cancer." Thousands of people will hear of my miracle and rejoice in Him. Despite my physical weakness, I continue to go to church to receive strength by worshipping Him. At times, it is difficult to have the energy to get my clothes and makeup on, and to get to church; but, God is helping me continuously. Having lived in this city for more than 46 years, God has given us much influence with thousands of people. Our church believes in the supernatural—signs, wonders, and miracles. You could say all of our eggs are in one basket—our faith and trust in Jesus Christ.

As I write this, our nation and our world have been turned upside down, and millions of people have died from the virus. A new term—"social distancing"—and wearing masks are the new norm. Though we are back in our physical church building, worshipping God, we are following CDC guidelines during our gatherings. My heart is always for and with people, and it is difficult not to be close and fellowship with them.

One of the highlights this summer was seeing my granddaughter Olivia graduate from high school with high honors, as well as being able to attend her graduation party. She is an anointed vessel of God and will be greatly used in His Kingdom. Soon she will be leaving to attend ministry school at The Ramp in Hamilton, Alabama. The school was started by Karen Wheaton and is training hundreds of young people for Kingdom ministry. We will certainly miss her; I love our fun times of shopping together, getting a coffee, or eating lunch. God is directing her path, and for that, we're thankful. She will carry on my legacy as another strong woman speaking the message of God's Kingdom.

During the month of July, I have been hospitalized three times with a bad case of colitis, high blood pressure, and a high thyroid number. After four weeks of declining health, not getting much sleep, I returned to Toledo Hospital on July 29th. For whatever reason, I wasn't able to eat very much during this month, and my body was getting weak. The surgeon wanted to have a feeding tube inserted to try building up strength in my body. While waiting to be taken back, the nurse was preparing me and heard Tony praying. What a touching moment as she joined in our prayer. The surgeon advised us that once he got into my stomach, there could be cancer and he would not be able to do anything further.

When I woke up, my first question was: "Did you find any cancer in my stomach?"

He replied, "No, no cancer; no issues whatsoever."

During all of my hospital stays, I have met dozens of healthcare workers. Some of them are definitely called and gifted while others are there performing a service. After I got out of the hospital, I sent out a tweet: "To God be the glory! Through it all, I've learned to trust in Jesus, I've learned to trust in God, I've learned to depend upon His Word."

From the book of Genesis, we learn the seasons of life go on continuously. Later, the Bible talks about a time to plant, a time to harvest, a time to rejoice, and a time to die. Cancer is a process from beginning to end, and Tony and Melony have been by my side every step of the way. I was cognizant of the Presence of Jesus even in my most difficult times. I knew He loved me, and live or die, I was secure in my faith.

This is one of my favorite psalms, Psalm 91:1-4, 9-10 (AMPC):

He who dwells in the Secret Place of the Most High shall remain stable and fixed under the shadow of the Almighty [Whose power no foe can withstand]. I will say of the Lord, He is my Refuge and my Fortress, my God; on Him I lean and rely, and in Him I [confidently] trust! For [then] He will deliver you from the snare of the fowler and from the deadly pestilence. [Then] He will cover you with His pinions, and under His wings shall you trust and find refuge; His Truth and His faithfulness are a shield and a buckler.

Because you have made the Lord your refuge, and the Most High your dwelling place, there shall no evil befall you, nor any plague or calamity come near your tent.

My heart is passionate for those who serve God in His Kingdom as messengers of His Truth. This is an article I wrote specifically dealing with women in ministry. However, it is for everyone.

Live your highest life—I want that for you. I pray that for you, I know where you are. I've been there; I've been in that box! But I also know where you're going—and living free to be who you are in Christ is the highest life! Don't be concerned about what people say or their actions. Keep your relationship with God strong and feel the Holy Spirit's Presence in your life. Be who you really are—don't be fake, be 100 percent yourself in Christ. See yourself the same as everyone else sitting in church. God loves you; He made us in His image, and you can be assured He's working on us every day. As a leader, I know we are to be godly examples, and we must always strive to do and live our best so our testimony will be effective. I've made many mistakes in my life; I've done things wrong, but I tried to always learn from my mistakes and to do better the next time. Through life's experiences, whether good or bad, God is teaching us something. He's making us better. That's one good reason to get older—you're always getting better and wiser. Things that once bothered me don't even get my attention now.

Take it from someone who's been there. Break free! Live your highest life in Christ, be who He made you to be, and serve Him in your own individual calling while loving

every minute of it. We must rest, relax, recreate, renew.
It's God's way of sustaining us for the long haul. We must
pray for our ministry responsibilities. Let God perform the
work, using His infinite strength and perfect wisdom. We
don't earn God's blessings by the amount of church work
we do. He wants us to lead healthy, balanced lives, where
ministry service is a joy and source of deep personal fulfillment. In the absence of such joy, ministry turns into burden
and burnout.

This writing came during the time of her most severe physical
challenges. Even then, Shirley was thinking of helping others to live
their highest life.

Returning home from Toledo Hospital, we were both encouraged that the feeding tube would give her the nutrients her body was
starving for. Daily, I would monitor her intake and slowly increase
the dosage to maximize the benefits. It is possible I was overly
optimistic that we would get the upper hand in this battle. Over the
next few days, she didn't sleep very well and at times only an hour
or two at night. We were battling high blood pressure, a high thyroid
number, pain, and malnutrition. Chemo had to be suspended for the
time being until she could regain her strength. By Friday, August 7th,
it became obvious that her health was declining. When I came to
bed that night, we held hands and believed together that she could
sleep. About 11:30 p.m., she woke me up to say that she was having
trouble breathing. I got up and dressed, dressed her, and we drove to
the hospital in Perrysburg. Immediately, they gave her oxygen and
pulled blood for the lab. They discovered her sodium level was 15 and
normal is 35. The attending physician suggested we transport her to
Toledo Hospital. We arrived there at about 1 a.m. and were placed in
a receiving area until a room opened for us. An hour or so later, we
moved her into a room, and they sedated her, so she could sleep. On

Monday, the doctor advised me that her sodium level was improving, but her lungs seemed to be inflamed, possibly from pneumonia. Her breathing was becoming more difficult, and I was told she needed a breathing tube in order to survive. She was sedated, not knowing it was going to be put in, and she was upset about it after waking up from the procedure. She could not speak with the breathing tube, so we began to write notes back and forth.

She wrote on the pad: "Am I dying?"

I said, "No, you are not. You are getting better."

The breathing tube was very uncomfortable, and they needed to keep her sedated during that week. I spent more than 21 hours a day at the hospital, and toward the weekend, she was noticeably getting worse. Never during any of this time, did I think she was going to die.

Not certain of her treatment, I requested a lung specialist to examine her. He came in and said he agreed with everything being done for her. On the weekend, I would leave her only for the time church was in session. After services, I would return immediately, spending every night with her. During my absence, Melony was there with her, so she always had someone to comfort her. At the conclusion of the 11 a.m. service on Sunday, August 16th, Melony called to say they were scheduling an emergency surgery. I raced as fast as I could to get there. The doctors were afraid her colon would rupture because there was a backup into her intestines. After having prayed with her, Melony and I went out to the waiting room. Several hours later, the surgeon made us aware of the challenges she faced. Things did not look good as I sat by her bed on Sunday night. Because of the heavy sedation following the surgery and the breathing tube, there was no communication, not even notes.

The following day, when she opened her eyes and looked at me, I could almost feel her questions:

"What is going on? What is happening to me?"

I assured her she was going to be better and soon the breathing tube would be taken out. I held her hand on Monday night until she went to sleep under heavy sedation. At about 1 a.m. in the morning, I was awakened by several people in the room and noticed her blood pressure was very low. The nurse informed me they were having trouble regulating her blood pressure, and it was continuing to drop. Eventually, there were five or six people working with her, and things did not look good. I called a friend, an elder of theChurch, Jon Harris, who lives just down the block from us. I asked him to pick up Melony from her house and bring her to the hospital.

Once there, she ran down the hall and fell into my arms, and with tears, she asked, "What is happening?"

By then, they had resuscitated Shirley several times and asked if I wanted them to try again. I said, "No."

At 4:05 a.m. on Tuesday morning, August 18th, Shirley passed into the arms of Jesus, slipping from the bonds of human flesh and becoming a spirit-being in the Third Heaven. Melony and I stood by her bed, commended her into the arms of Jesus, and drove to theChurch. We sat in the auditorium and prayed for some time and then returned home. My world was upside down. How could this be? Someone so loving, so kind, so generous, the most perfect pastor's wife, someone who loved God with all her heart, loved her family and loved her church was now gone. She wasn't the only one who left the world that day. A part of me went with her. That day I became a dead man walking. Shirley wasn't just my wife; she was my life. Next to God, there was no one and nothing that I loved more. Unquestionably, she was the best part of me. Shirley made me who I am today.

For a few days, I was like a zombie, praying the nightmare would end and we would continue our life and be back to normal. Many people speak of the five steps of grief and put confidence in the formula. Those five steps didn't work for me. Since I have never believed God is fragile, I bombarded Him with my questions. For sure, I did not agree with His decision to take her into Heaven. Everything I knew about God, His Word, Jesus, the Blood, the Cross, and the Resurrection told me to trust Him for her healing. "When the Healing Doesn't Come" is a good song, but it's not good theology for me. Throughout our years, I told Shirley God would take me before her because He knew I couldn't live without her. Certainly, she knew that also. To this day, I continue to process what has happened. My pain is too deep for words. My days are filled with tears, my nights are lonely, and I long for her presence. Now I have to prepare for life after Shirley. With us, it has always been **One + One = One**. Now, it's **One — One = One**.

The year 2020 turned our world upside down. It will take years to recover from the losses incurred by the virus. The downturn in the economies of the world, the deaths, schools being closed, businesses going under, and stresses of family life all took their toll on daily living. All I know is what God tells me—He makes all things beautiful in His time. Out of adversity and trial, God will bring blessing. In all things, we are taught that He works for our good. Those are things I will never stop believing. One of the greatest truths I have learned about life is summed up in these words—regardless of what happens, life goes on.

Since she was 15, Shirley has been my life. After three years of dating, we enjoyed 55 years of the treasure of married love. Along the way, we learned the covenant of oneness. Coming to approach life from a Kingdom perspective was one of our most memorable learning moments. God has a Kingdom on Earth, and His Kingdom operates on the basis of laws. Once you know those laws and live by them, you have the opportunity for the highest possible life. She and I became Kingdom covenant servants. We longed for, desired, and hungered for more knowledge for how His Kingdom worked. The Bible refers to this Kingdom as mysterious and even calls it secret.

Literally, you have to dig it out. It was this revelation from God that kept us through the years and is helping me now.

To this day, I have been processing her loss and my grief through my humanity—mind, will, and emotions. God prefers that all things in our life be processed by the laws of His Kingdom. He says, "We do not grieve as those who have no hope." My healing will come as I apply the law of grieving with hope.

Often, we had to live in times when the answers didn't come. Faced with questions for which I had no answers, I leaned hard on God, on my faith, on prayer. The road ahead is arduous, filled with pain, and at times I am overwhelmed with my grief. Always it was the two of us becoming one. Suddenly, I realized I don't know how to live without her. Intelligent, street smart, witty, funny, charming, she was the most loving person I've ever known. She not only was the love of my life, she was the life of my love. Today, I miss that incredible smile that could light up a room. Her ability to lift and encourage others was unsurpassed. Her life was filled with empathy for those who were struggling, wounded. And yes, I still ask God the question, "Why?"

This is the critical moment in the Christian faith where some people allow their doubts to overcome their belief system. As a pastor, I have witnessed people leave the church, abandon serving God, and go back to a life of sin because on the surface their prayers were not answered. There is no passage of Scripture that tells me God is obligated to answer every prayer I pray—even the most import-ant ones. The passage in Hebrews 11 has always been a great blessing to me during these times. It simply says that he who comes unto God must first believe that God is, and He is a rewarder of those who diligently seek His face. The most critical need in a

When you lack understanding at any given moment in your life, never abandon your faith— there is no better way to deal with life than to have faith in God.

relationship with Christ comes from Proverbs 4:7 (NKJV), "In all your getting, get understanding." Today, I am still confused as to why this happened, but I will never stop searching for the understanding, and I will never stop worshiping God. It's like Peter in John 6 when Jesus said to him, "Will you also go away?" To that question, Peter responded, "To whom shall we go? You have the Words of eternal life." When you lack understanding at any given moment in your life, never abandon your faith—there is no better way to deal with life than to have faith in God.

This side of Heaven, there will be no understanding of her loss. Surely the world needs more people like her. When she entered the Presence of Jesus, I was left with many questions about Heaven— Where is she? Who is there? What are they doing? These questions caused me to research and study every verse in the Bible about this place called Paradise. For more than four months, I have shared these powerful Truths with our church family. Heaven is more real to me today than ever before. Now I know Heaven and Earth are joined together while I live here on Earth. My life perspective has been transformed. Every day spent on the Earth is a day preparing to live eternally—whether it's in Heaven or...the other place. Paul even suggests we are preparing our wedding garments for the Marriage Supper of the Lamb (found in Revelation 20). A recording angel has been assigned the task of writing the life story we are dictating by our deeds, actions, and words (Malachi 3:16). There is no escaping the fact, the Truth, God wants us to live on Earth with a heavenly mindset. In reality, you can't be so heavenly-minded that you are of no earthly good. As you become heavenly-minded, you more completely fulfill your purpose in His Kingdom on Earth. And the good news is, you can start where you are today and get it right. No one ever expects to start their life over again; and yet, that is what I'm forced to do. Mind you, I didn't get a vote here. Truly, I expected God's Word of healing to work. Having lived my life on the basis of complete trust in His Word,

I was now faced with the consequence of not getting an answer. The question of "why" was not the only one.

Daily, I have to ask myself:

Where do I go from here?

How do I start over without her?

How can life ever really be worth living without her presence?

How long before the pain of this grief ceases?

Now I am confronted with a new formula of life for which I am not prepared to live: **One — One = One.**

Oneisms from Chapter 11

- ♥ Perseverance and determination are necessary to win the battle.

- ♥ Be cognizant of the Presence of Jesus even in your most difficult times. Know He loves you, and live or die, be secure in your faith.

- ♥ God is not fragile, and He can handle all of your questions.

- ♥ All I know is what God tells me—He makes all things beautiful in His time.

- ♥ Out of adversity and trial, God will bring blessing. In all things, we are taught He works for our good.

- ♥ Faced with questions for which you have no answers, lean hard on God, on faith, on prayer.

- ♥ In all of your getting, get understanding.

Chapter 12

One − One = One

ONE — One = **One** is a very difficult equation to adjust to. Truth is, I don't want to adjust to it. In reality, I want my life back—I want her back. Someone will read this and perhaps think how ridiculous such statements are. However, those are my thoughts, and I'm quite sure they will not change. **One** + **One** = **One** became our way of life. No couple we ever knew could have enjoyed being together as much as we did. While many people look for a formula to grieve with, I look for a scriptural position on grief. The Bible simply says we "do not grieve like the rest of mankind, who have no hope" (1 Thessalonians 4:13 NIV). Grief is not a choice, but it is forced upon us because of a loss. One morning at 4 a.m., I was awakened and pondered the grieving condition of my soul. Suddenly, a light came on, and I began to realize the greatest source of pain in my loss.

I have suffered the loss of her tangible love. Shirley loved me unreservedly, unconditionally, and with a passion too deep for words. Today, I am no longer experiencing the edifying, energizing, warmth, and affirmation of that love. With us, our love was never a surface thing. Now, there is a void, and nothing can fill it. On the one hand, I was blessed, enriched, enlarged, and increased in value by the power of her love. Her love for me didn't have to be repeated in words, since it was daily expressed in just being with her. This was a God kind of love, a selfless love, and a love based solely on our worth to each other. When you have experienced that kind of love, there is nothing that can replace it. For me, the definition of pure love is Shirley. Her love defined me. There is an old adage that says, "Don't cry because it's over, smile because it happened." I'm not there yet, perhaps I never will be.

Once again after many decades, I find myself asking these same questions while searching for the answers: Who Am I? What am I? Why am I? I am not who I was, I am not what I was, and I am not why I was. The loss of her love has forced upon me a new path of life. When we speak of a rebirth, a new beginning, a starting over, it is easier said than done. Shirley is woven into the fabric of my life so much that I still live by our routines. On Friday mornings, we always pulled the bedsheets to be laundered. It was my job to get them into the laundry room and her job to wash them. To this day, I still do these things on Friday mornings. On Saturday mornings, I gathered all of our clothes that needed to be washed and took them to the laundry room. She would always sort them into piles, and together during the day we would move them to hangers or the dryer.

Shirley was always meticulously clean, and everything had to be in its place before we went to bed. She never liked anything on top of the counters but inside the cabinets, unless it was decorative. Maybe these things seem small to you, but they are huge to me. You see, I'm determined to keep her alive in my heart and in my daily living. There is no reason to bore you with all the other things, but each day these routines and practices are a part of my life.

She was a woman of excellence no matter what she was involved in. Now it is **One — One** = **One**. On a daily basis, I wear the clothes she chose for me. Certain shirts go with certain sweaters, along with a choice of pants. Before ever leaving the house, I'm always cognizant of what she would want me to look like. More than once, I would hear her say, "I want you to be your best; I want you to look your best." Forever, she was thinking about me, loving me, and now forever, I am thinking about her, minus that tangible love. What you are reading in this book is my attempt to honor the place she occupied in my life. At no time in our 58 years, did I feel like I deserved her. Actually, I counted myself as fortunate, blessed because God put her in my life. It is my goal to finish my life having honored God, honored my wife, honored my children, and honored His Kingdom. May God help me to never bring dishonor to any of those.

During our years of traveling (and we traveled around the world), she chose special places, and we returned to them often. Hilton Hawaiian Village was the one place she loved more than any other. It is possibly one of the most beautiful scenes on Earth. As of today, I don't believe I could ever go there again. Memories from the past flood my mind of all the things we would do together.

In 2017, even though she had been sick for almost a year, she insisted on climbing Diamond Head. That climb is straight up the mountain on a very narrow trail. Of course, I begged her not to do that hike, but she insisted on going. And go, she did. She was a very strong woman and pursued life with a spirit of adventure. Another one of our favorite places was Huntington Beach, California. Stunning sunsets captivated our attention late in the afternoon as we sat by the beach. Our oneness was such that we didn't have to constantly talk to each other—just being with her and seeing her smile as she watched the sun disappear into the ocean was enough. And once again, that is a destination I don't think I can return to. Going forward, I am going to be minus her input with all the projects we discussed and planned to expand the ministry and outreach of theChurch.

Currently, we are in the planning stages of a new assisted living care facility that will honor her legacy. This is where she would truly shine because of her attention to detail and excellence. Her love and care for people would offer residents an experience like no other. Our stunning campus has been kept immaculate for 15 years because of her diligence to maintain it. Any time we needed to replace carpet, chairs, tables, or to repaint, she insisted on an interior decorator helping with the project. When meeting with the new facility project head, my heart breaks that she is not here to give input. Yet, it will be named after her, and it will continue her legacy of caring deeply for those who need assistance on their life's journey. Her favorite hymn was "It Is Well." My granddaughter Olivia took her grandmother's handwriting and got a tattoo on her forearm with those very words. Melony saw it and did the same to honor her mother. Naming the center after her is only possible because she is not here. Shirley never wanted attention focused on herself.

Because we are still one, and forever will be, I am constantly aware of what she would want. Often people coin a certain phrase to define how they live life. For Shirley, it was "simple elegance." Actually, any time you saw her, those words fit her own appearance. Whatever clothes she wore, the outfits would be simply elegant. Throughout her lifetime, she lived in such a way to define class—she was one class act! No one loved more, cared more, or gave more to make other people's lives better than she did. To say that she was the heart and soul of our ministry would simply be an understatement.

One of her great attributes was learning the story of someone she had just met. Her love for people, especially those hurting and wounded, knew no limits. Their story was always important to her. As I view my life today and look toward the future, my greatest challenge is to live up to the standard she set with her life. Before her chemo treatments and surgery in 2018, she had scheduled a Friday Women's Worship Night. Although weakened from losing so much weight, she insisted on doing the meeting. It was almost 10 p.m. when she arrived home, and she could hardly get into the house because of the weakness of her body. I helped her get ready for bed and asked why she was so late. She told me there were many women at the meeting who wanted help, and she prayed for them individually. All the while, she was standing on her feet. And that was Shirley—unselfish, caring, loving, tender, and always putting others and their needs first.

In all of the messages God helped me to do, she was the one who helped me polish them. Every week, she would read the written manuscript, word for word, and challenge me on something I was going to say. At times, she would question a word, even if it came straight from the Bible.

"Is there a better way to say this?" she would ask. "Do you really have to include this?"

Sometimes, it would create a disagreement, and I would be challenged to justify my statements. There are no words to describe what she meant to me. Simply put, she was my life, and I miss those discussions and her strong spirit. Whatever I have been able to achieve in my ministry calling is largely responsible from her coaching me, believing in me, challenging me, motivating me, but most of all—loving me.

Now, our family must contend with the new equation: **One — One = One**. My son and daughter, along with our four granddaughters, could have no greater example of the Christian life than Shirley's. Her in-your-face, yet kind and loving style could penetrate any barrier. Always wanting each of us to be our best, she would speak her mind in any given situation. Her strength of courage, her Christian character, her love of Jesus, her commitment to His Kingdom were evident in her words and her actions. No mother loved her children more than she did. And yet, regardless of their age, she would still correct them in what she perceived to be questionable actions and deeds. Melony, Olivia, Bella, Mackenzie, and Abbie were given a role model par excellence on being a woman, being strong, being a leader, and doing it all with class and excellence. Melony,

Olivia, and Mackenzie have a great future in ministry because of how Shirley loved and excelled in it. Whatever she put her mind and hand to was always done with excellence. Never a quitter, she would find a way, in spite of challenges, to get the job done. As discouraging as life in ministry can be at times, that never stopped her from giving it her best effort. I realize what a loss we have all suffered. Actually, the world has suffered the loss of one of the greatest people who ever walked this Earth. Although we know there are no perfect people, she was as close to one as it gets. Her love was real, her passion was moving, her effort was flawless, and her achievements were excellent. The question for all of us becomes, how do we take what she has shown us about life and implement it into our daily walk with Christ? For her, to live was Christ, His Kingdom, her family, His church. No one I knew loved life more than she.

One — One = **One** is the only fitting way to speak of us now. While gone from our physical presence, she will always be with us in spirit. Those who knew and loved her will never forget the contagious beauty of her smile, the effervescent look of joy on her face, and the genuineness of her warmth and hugs. Her laughter came from deep within her soul and was never shallow or superficial. It could be felt deeply, it was real, full of energy, and it caused those around her to laugh as well.

For 58 years, we were one. **One + One** = **One**. Our covenant of oneness is eternal for me. One wife for all of life and eternity as well. Though she is gone from the Earth, I am still one with her. As long as I live, she will be alive, because I will never allow her to be forgotten. To her great-grandchildren, I will speak of the beauty, the glory of her life. From me, they will hear the stories of how she impacted others and caused them to want to be the best version of themselves. To know Shirley was to love her and love her I did.

Not only did I love her, but she was also loved by thousands of people the world over. Even with her passing into Heaven, she wanted the focus on worship to Jesus. Her specific instructions were:

Have a regular worship service and celebrate my life.
Let Jesus be worshiped: no casket,
no funeral home, no funeral service.
Speak of what Jesus did for me and through me.

On the outside lawn of the church campus, we erected two 500-seat tents with 1000 plus chairs. On that special "celebration of life" day, the chairs were filled and thousands joined us online. The service lasted over two hours and not one person left early. Even in her graduation to Heaven, Shirley mesmerized people with her life. People drove from hundreds of miles away or flew in to honor her. For her "celebration of life" service, we knew she wanted simple elegance, and that is what we attempted to do. No one who attended will ever forget that day or the beauty of a life well-lived.

After the celebration of life service, I was confronted by the huge desire to know where she was. Until this time in my life, I had spent very little effort researching Heaven. Just knowing I would go there someday was simply enough for me. While many people say there isn't a lot in the Bible about Heaven, I actually discovered there is much information about where it is, who is there, what's going on, and the amazing worship that is taking place at this precise moment. I especially wanted to know what happened to Shirley when she took her last breath in this life.

Did she immediately go into the Presence of Jesus?
Leaving her flesh behind, what form did she take on?
What is she doing?

As I prayed, studied, and researched, Heaven took on a new meaning. More than ever before, I thirst for knowledge of this place called Paradise. Let me state the obvious: there is no question that Shirley went directly into the Presence of Jesus in Heaven to a place called Paradise. Beginning with the week of her passing, I have not ceased researching the biblical teachings on the habitation of those who die in the Lord. You need to know some of the things I have discovered about our eternal home.

Selfishly, this Heaven series was more for me, but God used it to help so many people who also face the grieving process. Heaven is an actual place, a realm where the "Grand Central Station" of the Kingdom of God operates. The apostle Paul calls it the Third Heaven, or Paradise. Paradise refers to a walled-in garden of beauty and magnificence. Kings of the orient would often have such beautiful gardens and entertain sovereigns from other nations. At the precise moment believers take their last breath, a blink of an eye, they pass into the Presence of Jesus. There is no such thing as soul sleep, a state of death, a place of waiting. As fast as you blink your eye, you are in the Presence of Jesus. Theologically speaking, you become a disembodied spirit-being. On the Mount of Transfiguration, God gives us a picture of this. Moses and Elijah appeared there with Jesus in their spirit-being forms. Interestingly, they discussed with Him things He was about to experience on Earth, which tells us those in Heaven know what's going on in God's Kingdom on Earth. Around the Throne of God, in the realm of Heaven, there is unceasing worship. When worshiping God on Earth, we join with the great throng of angels and departed saints in Heaven. As to where Heaven is...it's a realm just above the Earth. Jesus stepped into the clouds and was immediately in Heaven. The distance to Heaven is not measured in light-years (how far light travels in a year—about six trillion miles), but in degrees of awareness. While it is true death is the one thing to separate us from Heaven at this very moment, we should have no fear of it. Believers don't die, they just transition into Heaven. In a sense, it is not "leaving home" but "going home." The stronger your belief in Heaven, the more confidence you have in facing life's challenges on Earth. Heaven is a prepared place for a prepared people. While on Earth, God is preparing us to live eternally with Him. Our willingness to be obedient to His commands conditions us, readies us, qualifies us, to rule and reign with Him in Heaven and on Earth. Paul declares we are preparing the garments that we will wear at the Marriage Supper of the Lamb (in Ephesians 5). The degree to which you live with a heavenly mindset determines the degree to which you live victoriously while on Earth. As I became aware of these things, knowing where Shirley was and what she was doing, a great comfort came into my spirit. Since there will be no marriages in Heaven, we will be as the angels. Yet, I will know her, and she will know me. Whether we will have knowledge of our life on Earth, I cannot say at this time. One thing I know for certain...when I arrive in Heaven, I want to see Jesus, and then I will look, and there she will be. What it means to "know as we are known" I am not certain of at this moment, but I will know her, and she will know me. We will be His children, and we will serve Him once again together in His eternal Kingdom. My prayer is that angels have close friends because I am not going to let her out of my sight. The greatest motivation I have for Heaven while I am here on this Earth is that Shirley is there. While I am left here to live out my years on the Earth minus her tangible love, I am trying to adjust to **One — One = One**.

Winter seasons can often be very challenging, very dark, and very cold. It is a time when things die. Many years ago on a trip to Israel, I remarked to our guide about the barrenness of the land with rocks everywhere.

I said to him, "Where is your dirt?"

He replied, "Do you know where dirt comes from?"

While I really didn't know, I said, "Sure, I do!"

He told me that story of the Romans cutting down all the trees in order to cause death to the nation of Israel. With no trees dying, no grass, no shrubs or bushes, no new anything, dirt accumulates. And after hundreds of years, civilizations cease to exist. If there is no dirt, there are no seeds, there is no harvest. It was a powerful teaching moment for me about the necessity of a winter season. Through the process of death, God brings new life. The winter season actually creates the minerals to enrich the soil to produce a harvest in the fall. As much as I despair my "winter seasons," I am truly thankful for what they produce in my life. Truly, the passing of Shirley into the arms of Jesus has become a winter season for me. At the writing of this book, I know not what the harvest might be.

Sometimes, when it looks like we are losing, we are actually winning. The book of Daniel is a powerful illustration of this truth. After earnestly seeking God for an answer, his prayers continued for for 21 days. An angel arrived to let him know God heard him on the first day he prayed. He was delayed in the heavenlies by a messenger of Satan. Daniel was fasting during this time and in a weakened physical condition. It really looked like he was losing, but he was actually winning. The angel gave him understanding of things to come in the future. It was a powerful prophetic Word that could not be revealed at that time. Even to this day, that Word is shared throughout God's Kingdom. What a great victory! And so it is with us.

Never forget that God knows where you are, what you're going through, and how you are responding to life every single day. He has already been in your tomorrow and made it safe for you to go there. Though you know not what tomorrow holds, live with confidence that no matter what you face, you and God are a majority. While life may not always make sense, God always does. Never forget that your life is a poem, it's a work of art, you are His piece of work. Whatever you put in His hands will be returned to you in its most blessed form. Never surrender something to Him and then pick it back up. While you may not totally understand He is sovereign, you should know He planned for you to live your highest life. He will never give up on that and neither should you. While **One — One** = **One** is not a truth any of us want to experience, our faith in God tells us it is not over. With every circumstance of life, you can know this truth—your story doesn't end with what happens. It ends with what God does with what happens to you.

The sovereignty of God cannot be questioned and yet my soul demands an answer for how such a warm, wonderful, wise, witty, loving person could be taken from the Earth. When God commanded us in all of our getting to get understanding, He knew life would not always make sense. Some do not understand why I don't agree with His decision to take Shirley. My only excuse is my humanity, my flesh. Never did I think our wonderful equation, given by God, of **One** + **One** = **One** would one day become **One** — **One** = **One**. There is no passage of Scripture that guarantees we will understand the ways of God. However, the Psalmist said, "He made known His ways to Moses." You remember Moses didn't agree with God's decision to wipe out the Israelites and said so. I state my case. If Moses could disagree with the decision, perhaps God in His mercy will permit me to as well. While I don't have all the answers, and my loss is greater than my words can express, that will never diminish my faith in the God I serve, Who gave me the greatest treasure in my life—ShirleyAnn Lesley Scott. Still one, always one, forever one.

The truth and principles that she and I lived out in our 58 years together are written on the pages of this book. The laws and principles of His Word are the only foundation upon which to build any relationship. We filled this book with them, so you can live your highest life of oneness. Our prayer is for you to experience the blessing, the treasure, of covenant love, and be loved for the value of yourself. In God's mercy, may you have an incredible relationship words are not adequate to describe.

One + One = One

That is the world's greatest love relationship equation.

Oneisms from Chapter 12

- ♥ Grief is not a choice but is forced on us because of a loss.

- ♥ Find a God kind of love, a selfless love, a love based solely on the worth of each other.

- ♥ Whatever you put your mind and hand to, do it with excellence.

- ♥ The death of a spouse simply alters the equation to **One — One = One**.

- ♥ May you ever long to know about your forever life—Paradise.

- ♥ While it is true that death is the one thing that separates us from Heaven, we should have no fear of death.

- ♥ The stronger your belief in Heaven, the more confidence you have in facing life's challenges on Earth. Heaven is a prepared place for a prepared people.

- ♥ Our willingness to be obedient to His commands conditions us, readies us, qualifies us, to rule and reign with Him in Heaven and on Earth.

- ♥ The degree to which one lives with a heavenly mindset determines the degree to which you live victoriously while on Earth.

What Death Can't Steal From You

ONE — One = **One** is not a tragedy. It's the story of the most incredible love two people could experience. Our love is an eternal one that death cannot steal from us. She lives on through Darin, Melony, and her four granddaughters. Not a day goes by that someone hasn't contacted me concerning her impact on their life. The legacy she left is one of deep faith and trust in God's sovereignty, as well as the total use of her gift mix for His Kingdom.

Shirley lived a life without regrets. With a forgiving spirit, a tender heart, and empathy for the hurts of others, she became a role model for thousands of women who would come after her, seeing her devotion to God. From the Third Heaven, God's Paradise, she is still speaking to us with the life she lived on Earth. Her voice is heard through Darin, Melony, Olivia, Bella, Mackenzie, and Abbie on a daily basis. Because of her inspiration and her challenge to me that our dream would not die, the new assisted living care facility will be built to honor her. Our story will serve as a witness to many people about the power of covenant love. Death cannot steal from her the Christian legacy she created with her living. While tireless in her efforts for the Kingdom of God here on the Earth, she always held eternity in her heart. Today she is experiencing what she lived life to achieve—life in the very Presence of Jesus. Wherever you find yourself in life at this moment, she would want you to know three things:

Honor and serve God with your whole heart.

Love your family with His love.

Serve His Kingdom with your gifts, talents, and abilities.

Because I knew her love, I became a better person than I ever hoped to be. There are some things that death will never steal from me—the absolute joy, peace, and security her love gave me. And while death is an enemy, it cannot steal the legacy of a life well-lived. While I will never this side of Heaven understand why God did not heal her, I will obey His command found in Proverbs 4:7 (AMPC), "And with all you have gotten, get understanding (discernment, comprehension, and interpretation)."

Understanding is insight into the ways of God. He "made known His ways to Moses" and surely, He will do no less for us. Never be so focused on the answer you are seeking from God that you fail to see the one He is giving you. You were created to first be *one* with Him and only then will it be possible to experience the Law of Oneness with others.

Acknowledgments

ON our life's journey, ShirleyAnn and I have been enriched by God's special covenant people. Each of them made a deposit into us which made us more than we had become.

Lauren Clark: For your editing, amazing grammatical intelligence, and for crying with me while writing this book.

Jenny Schmidt: For working diligently on the website, marketing, and graphics. Phenomenal talent!

Ed Marroquin: For praying with me, encouraging me during the challenging times. Your video tributes to Shirley were beautiful. Thank you.

John and Lisa Harris: For inspiring us and supporting us with love, prayers, and resources.

Jess and Beth Saylor: For helping me bring the book to print and distribution.

Jeff and Kay Ziegler: For being true covenant friends who are helping us get this message out to thousands of people.

Peggy Otieno: For praying daily for me to heal from my grief. Shirley loved you dearly.

Melony Bradley: For simply being the best God-sent daughter a father and mother could have. Your administrative gifts kept the ministry thriving through all of our pain.

Olivia and Mackenzie Bradley: For our two granddaughters who bring me great joy as they wholeheartedly serve God.

Darin Scott: For our son who has always had a tender heart for God and an entrepreneurial, energetic spirit. You will thrive. We love you.

Bella and Abbie Scott: For our two granddaughters who have bright, creative personalities with God-loving hearts.

And of course, to ShirleyAnn Lesley Scott, the greatest gift of my life and the one who made me more than what I thought I could become. I love you forever!

About the Authors

TWO young kids growing up on mill villages just 30 miles apart would one day in the providence of God meet face-to-face. Tony and Shirley Scott came from very humble backgrounds, where their families had limited resources. Raised in homes where devotion to biblical principles were taught opened their hearts to God and His will for their lives. From the time they met at youth camp in their teens, until Shirley's homegoing, they pursued their purpose. Tony's desire to write and share powerful Kingdom principles started with his first book, *Living the Diamond Life in a Rocky World*. As they followed their journey, two more books were written by him—*The Increase Life* and *The Diamond Life: You Are More Than You Have Become*. The author has spoken in more than ten countries on five continents, relative to living a life of significance. His passion, as well as was hers, is to see people's purpose lived and to realize their highest life. ***One + One = One*** is the culmination of their experiences and their 58 years together.

ONE + ONE = ONE STUDY GUIDE

The interactive study guide is designed to take relationships to the next level. This study guide combined with the book can be used with individual couples and small group settings. It has the power to move any relationship to the next level.

THE DIAMOND LIFE

Your life is created as a diamond in the rough. The purpose of your life can only be revealed as you experience the Diamond Life Formula. You are to be shaped, cut, chiseled, refined, and polished in order for your true value and beauty to be seen. Read this and become who you really are!

TO PURCHASE, AND FOR FREE RESOURCES, VISIT
TONYSCOTT.TV